Finally, a devotional guide that paints the ~~g~~ ~~p~~
redemptive story. *90 Days Thru the Bible* masterfully covers the
biblical account from beginning to end in a way that not only
enlightens the reader but also connects God's story with the
work He's doing right now, in and through us. This book is
high-octane nourishment for Christians at all levels of spiritual
maturity.

**MEL SVENDSEN**
Lead pastor, Riverview Church, Bonsall, CA

If you want to read the story of the Bible, do not miss *90 Days
Thru the Bible*. It takes the story of the Bible, which many people
have learned through Walk Thru the Bible's live events—Walk
Thru the Old Testament or Walk Thru the New Testament—
and puts it into an easy-to-read and easy-to-understand story . . .
a simple narrative that will lead you through the major people,
places, and events in a way that will capture your imagination in
fresh and creative ways. In an age of biblical illiteracy, what an
awesome way to see and remember the greatest story of all time.

**STEVE KEYES**
Pastor

*90 Days Thru the Bible* is a beautifully written devotional that
provides a powerful and penetrating journey through God's Word
that enables the reader to draw from the depths of Scripture for
encouragement, strength, and wisdom for life application.

**LT. COL. KENNETH W. MAYNOR**
Territorial secretary for program, The Salvation Army

Many have said, "You can't see the forest for the trees." When
it comes to grasping God's message to us in the Bible, it's
important to see both the forest and the trees! *90 Days Thru the*

*Bible* helps us do just that. The writing gives us a clear picture of the overall message of the Bible and helps us see the particular truths of the Christian faith. Get this book!"

**KEITH MOORE**

Senior pastor, Dogwood Church, Tyrone, GA

# 90 Days Thru the Bible

A DEVOTIONAL JOURNEY FROM

WALK THRU THE BIBLE

with Chris Tiegreen

TYNDALE
MOMENTUM

*An Imprint of*
*Tyndale House Publishers, Inc.*

Visit Tyndale online at www.tyndale.com.

Visit Tyndale Momentum online at www.tyndalemomentum.com.

Visit Walk Thru the Bible at www.walkthru.org.

*Tyndale Momentum* and the Tyndale Momentum logo are trademarks of Tyndale House Publishers, Inc. Tyndale Momentum is an imprint of Tyndale House Publishers, Inc.

The Walk Thru the Bible logo is a registered trademark of Walk Thru the Bible Ministries, Inc.

*90 Days Thru the Bible: A Devotional Journey from Walk Thru the Bible*

**Library of Congress Cataloging-in-Publication Data**

Tiegreen, Chris.
  90 days thru the Bible : a devotional journey from Walk thru the Bible /
Chris Tiegreen.
    p. cm.
  ISBN 978-1-4143-5309-8 (sc)
1. Bible—Meditations. I. Title.
  BS491.5.T54 2012
  242´.5—dc23                                          2012015842

Printed in the United States of America

18   17   16   15   14   13   12
 7    6    5    4    3    2    1

# Table of Contents

*To John Fretz, Sandy Eidson, and Maggie Eldridge—with sincere gratitude for shepherding Walk Thru the Bible's live events for almost three decades. Because of your tireless efforts, more than two million people have a better understanding of the big picture of God's Word.*

*"For I know the plans I have for you," declares the LORD,*
*"plans to prosper you and not to harm you,*
*plans to give you hope and a future."*

JEREMIAH 29:11, NIV

# Introduction

One might think that the bestselling book of all time would be one of the most understood books of all time, but it isn't. Though many people have found inspiration in the pages of the Bible, far fewer have actually read it from beginning to end. Many have believed the overall message of the Bible, but few have grasped the entire story. That's because God's message is simple enough for a child to embrace, yet His epic story is complex enough to mystify even the most curious intellect. We grasp the pieces much more easily than we comprehend the whole.

Many people can recite the basic message of the Bible—God created a good world, human beings sinned and fell, and God eventually sent a solution in the form of His Son, who was offered as a sacrifice for sin and will one day return to rule—and many have learned important life principles from the lives of prominent biblical characters—faith from the life of Abraham, courage from the conflict between David and Goliath, compassion from the story of the Good Samaritan, forgiveness from the parable of the Prodigal Son. Meanwhile, huge portions of the Law and the Prophets—and even a few New Testament letters—remain largely untouched. Between the basic message and some of the well-known stories, deep, dark sections of Scripture remain obscure.

The pages of many Bibles are ruffled in predictable spots and pristine in equally predictable spots.

It's entirely possible, then, for us to be well versed in certain specifics and yet ignorant of major themes. We may know key doctrines of our faith—especially those favored by our particular denomination or historical tradition—and miss the heart of God. That in itself is a biblical phenomenon. Entire generations of God's people in Scripture became experts in their sacred writings but didn't recognize God's voice as spoken through the prophets; many missed the Messiah Himself because they studied Scripture through a certain lens and failed to comprehend the heart of it. We don't want to do that. We can't afford to proclaim the certainty of God's Word while remaining ignorant of huge sections of it. Our voices carry no weight when we declare that the God of the universe has revealed Himself in the Bible and simultaneously admit that we haven't actually read all of it. We far too often tend to ascribe glory to God's Word and then never get around to exploring it fully for ourselves.

This ninety-day devotional won't explore the Bible fully, of course; it's impossible to be that thorough in short daily readings. Rather, the purpose of this book is to draw the major themes out of each book of Scripture and to meditate on how each one contributes to God's great story. At one level, it's an overview, but it's designed to go much deeper than that—more like admiring the beauty of each piece of a puzzle and contemplating how it contributes to the whole picture. In the process, we will encounter the major characters, events, and themes of the Bible and discover a divine flow that connects them all. We will see how God unveiled Himself and His purposes over diverse centuries and through diverse people. The majesty of Scripture will inspire us more deeply and enhance our appreciation of the heart of God.

Underneath this journey through Scripture, underlying even the Bible's very existence, is a truth often unacknowledged in this world: *God speaks*. He is not silent. By implication, this also means He is neither distant nor indifferent. He is not the cosmic Creator who wound the world up like a clock and then left it to run on its own. He is not an "absentee landlord," as some have charged. No, God is a communicator. He has desires and purposes and answers to impart. He wants to be known.

That's a landmark truth, and when we realize its implication—that not only does God speak, but He speaks *to us*—our interest is piqued and our lives are changed. Every human being with any instinct that God exists knows what it's like to pray to Him and desperately wait for His responses. The entire world seeks truth. The simple knowledge that our God is not silent and that He has revealed Himself not only to the world as a whole but also to us as individuals is an alluring thought that sends us in search of answers. We want to know more. We know we need His Word, if only we can understand it.

This book will explore the Word that has been revealed. It won't cover every detail, summarize every story, or mention every character; we have to read the Bible itself for that. But it will help us understand the often-obscure collection of inspired writings comprised by Scripture, and it will illuminate huge, life-altering themes that give our lives meaning. Somewhere in the process, we will hear the voice of the One who speaks.

DAY 1

# THE OLD TESTAMENT

The Old Testament can be intimidating, not only because of its size, but also because of its complexity. Some of its stories seem simple, but the lists of laws and rituals and the chronicles of kings and prophets—many of them not presented in chronological order—make for dense reading. Beneath the surface are layers upon layers of meaning that we don't see. The heart of the story can get lost in the details, as can the God who authored it.

When reading the Old Testament story, it's important to look at the way certain characters and themes develop. We see human beings, made in the image of God, become rebels and then wanderers. Out of these disconnected people, God chooses a man, gives him a family, and then grows his family into a nation. After the nation is chosen and cultivated, the people are disciplined harshly for years because they give their hearts to lesser gods, but then they are restored—all of which sets the context for and leads up to a supernaturally new creation.

We can see a story line with God, too—first as Creator, then as Judge, and as powerful Lord. But His more personal characteristics begin to come through as He shows Himself to be a Deliverer, Redeemer, Healer, and Provider. As the story continues, we see God portray Himself not only as Master but also as a gentle Shepherd and a compassionate Father. In the New Testament, this progression of intimacy continues all the way to Friend and then Bridegroom. Again and again, God pursues closeness with His people. What began as a rescue turned into a courtship, a betrothal, and eventually a marriage between the human and the divine. There are times of separation, the greatest of which—an exile—occupies the attention of many of the prophets.

But chastisement is only one side of God's love, and certainly not the dominant side. Throughout the Old Testament, God wants His presence to be known among His people. This connection was broken with the Fall, but the distance was bridged by God's presence in a Tabernacle and then a Temple, and the prophets foretold a time when it would get much closer than that. In every instance, God reveals Himself very personally as someone who zealously wants to be known.

This relationship is a partnership, too, with a mission that begins at Creation—to fill the earth and subdue it—and continues with God's people being set apart for Him as a nation of priests for the world, a light that reflects His glory, and bearers of His truth. This mission develops into a full-blown Kingdom agenda that, at the end of Scripture, involves our not only serving God, but also ruling with Him. This is a God with a purpose.

Central to this purpose, the key to the rescue, is the sacrificial death of God made manifest in human flesh, Jesus Christ. The Crucifixion wasn't a backup plan; it was God's way to achieve His desire for ultimate closeness with *us*, His creation. God's saving work through the promised Messiah can be seen in virtually every book of Hebrew Scripture—in symbols, signs, and stories, and in living parables that God arranged but whose participants could not have known what they were representing. Everything in Scripture points either toward the coming Messiah (Old Testament) or to the risen and living Lord (New Testament). He is the centerpiece of God's story—God Himself stepping personally into the world He created.

But before God, in flesh and blood, steps into human history, He prepares the way over the course of centuries. He works through His people, speaks through His prophets, and lays out pieces of His plan. He calls and cultivates, chastens and refines, and progressively reveals glimpses of His true nature. Over time, He draws all of His people back to Him.

## Questions for Reflection

What first comes to mind when you think of the Old Testament? How important do you think it is to our understanding of the New Testament? Why?

 DAY 2

# GENESIS 1–3

In a sense, the whole Bible is contained in the book of Genesis. Granted, much of it is veiled—there are only subtle hints of God's plan of redemption and His ultimate purpose for humanity—but the scope of Scripture is remarkably foreshadowed by the fifty chapters of Genesis. The seeds of every major facet of our faith are planted here. We read of a Creator who was greatly pleased with His original creation; we learn why life is so hard now; we get profound pictures of our own struggles in the lives of the people portrayed; we glimpse the big-picture plan of a God who has the whole world on His heart and a particular people in His strategy; we take comfort in the fact that God works through people of enormous dysfunction to accomplish His purposes; we see pictures of the One coming to redeem what was lost; we confront the fundamental questions of life.

Genesis gives us answers to those questions—not complete, systematic answers, but answers nonetheless. Whereas some religions view cosmic history as a never ending cycle of birth, death, and rebirth, and the nonreligious view it as purely a material existence, the Bible tells us that human life has a supernatural beginning, progresses in a linear fashion, and will reach a fulfilling climax that lasts for eternity. There is purpose and direction in this story. Our nagging questions—"Why are we here?" "What is the meaning of it all?" "If there is a God, what is He like?"—are all dealt with coherently. Genesis is the Rosetta stone of the human experience, the key that cracks the code on all the big questions. We still have some interpreting to do, and many details will be filled in later, but the template is there.

It begins with a voice—God's voice speaking into the dark nothingness and creating a vast universe that includes at least one small planet teeming with life. Like an artist's brush, the voice paints light and shadows, colors and continents and seas, plant life and animal life, and the right environment for life to thrive. Then, to form the crowning piece of creation, He breathes life into dust and puts His own image into human beings. At every stage of creation, the artist is pleased with His work. It is good—until He sees that the man is alone. That isn't good. So He creates a companion, another bearer of the image. Now, as male and female together, they reflect the strength and beauty, the power and grace, the conquering and nurturing aspects of God's own character. Human beings are told to fill the earth with plenty of offspring—more pictures of God's image—and to tame the wildness of the world. In other words, the beauty and order of Eden is meant to spread.

But instead of the goodness of the Garden spreading outward into the world, the chaos of rebellion wells up in the form of a deceptive serpent. The tempter casts shadows on God's goodness. Perhaps the good Creator is holding out on His image-bearers. Are they really like Him? Not if they don't have His knowledge, the serpent suggests. Not if He put really good-looking fruit right in front of them and told them not to eat it. Not if His words can be twisted enough to make it seem as if He is keeping secrets that would be good for them to know.

So they eat—first the woman, then the man. And the serpent was right. They know things. They see the distinction between good and evil. Now they can judge right and wrong, each other, and even God. History will now be filled with accusations against God's goodness, all because the image-bearers fell for a lie, invited evil into their own lives, and then turned their newfound ability to judge back at Him. Never mind that their perspective is limited; the world is broken, and they know it. And for generations to come, the bearers of a now-distorted image will wrestle with each other, the world, and the God who created it for allowing the pain and suffering that is now a part of their existence.

Even so, God has a plan. If we read closely enough, we sense that His reaction to the Fall is premeditated, that His plan was already in place. We're told much later in Scripture that the Lamb had been slain from the foundation of the world; the sacrifice for our rebellion was an eternal fact before our rebellion even happened. Just as God knows all our mistakes before we make them and weaves them into His purposes, He knew that this is how His world would turn, and He had already made provision. The rest of Scripture is the story of how that provision unfolds.

## Questions for Reflection

How did God demonstrate in Genesis that He had already planned a solution for humanity's fall? Do you think God already has solutions for the crises we face today? Why or why not?

 DAY 3

# GENESIS 4–11

The pages of Scripture between the Fall and the story of Abraham are few, but they cover thousands of years of human history. Life outside of Eden isn't pretty—brother kills brother; an entire generation becomes so evil that God feels compelled to wipe it out, except for a man named Noah and his family; another curse immediately follows the rescue in the ark, as one of Noah's sons exposes the shame of his father; and a prideful people on the plains of Shinar, one day to be known as Babylon, come together to make a name for themselves and ascend to godly heights. Their tower project is abandoned when God scrambles their languages. Babel becomes a symbol of the futility of human effort, the place where self-exalting plans are foiled. By God's design, history is filled with such frustrations. There is no way to get to God or solve our problems on our own.

We tend to think of the Bible primarily in terms of how it relates to us: what it tells us about ourselves, what it commands us to do, and so on. But it is first and foremost a revelation of God. Think of what God shows us about Himself in just the first eleven chapters of Genesis—primeval history from the moment of creation to God's choice of Abraham as a father of nations. God has incomprehensible power; His spoken words can create entire worlds. He takes great satisfaction in His works—every "it was good" in the Creation story makes that clear. He gets angry over evil and grieves its effects—the fiasco in the Garden of Eden and the events leading up to the Flood show us that. He gives us a sense of His "otherness" in the Creation story and in the fact that He has to "come down" to Babel to see humanity's highest accomplishment. And we see His foresight and His mercy in the fact that He has a redemption plan ready even before His image-bearers distort the image through the Fall. Even before evil's earliest intrusion into His creation, God demonstrates His relentless love. His nature breathes from the pages of this first book of Scripture.

We also learn a lot about ourselves from these first eleven chapters. We know, for example, that we are created in God's own image. In other words, we are uniquely designed to be able to relate to God intellectually, emotionally, and spiritually. We can connect with Him at the deepest levels of relationship. Why? Because God apparently wants to share who He is with creatures who can not only appreciate Him—angels can do that, too, to a degree—but also engage with Him in some semblance of a give-and-take dynamic.

We also know that this image was somehow fractured and damaged by human rebellion. Some aspect of our connection with God has been lost, and without it we sink deeper and deeper into skewed perceptions, twisted thoughts, misplaced emotions, and unseemly actions—all driven by a self-centered focus rather than a focus on God.

The result is that we forget the mission humanity was given in the Garden—to fill the earth and subdue it, to spread God's garden outward, to exercise dominion over a world that was once "formless and void"—and we begin pursuing our own agendas and missions. The tree of the knowledge of good and evil has given us heavy doses of independence; that's always a by-product of having confidence in our own knowledge. Carried away as wanderers and estranged from God, we subject ourselves to His opposition, not because He opposes *us*, but because He opposes the direction we have taken. He judges with a flood because of humanity's thorough corruption. He scatters at Babel because of humanity's attempt to unite and build a monument under the banner of self-made religion. In the first few chapters of Genesis, creation is clearly not fulfilling its purpose. Yet.

## Question for Reflection

In what ways does Genesis 4–11 reflect the truth of Romans 8:20-21?

DAY 4

# GENESIS 12–24

When primeval history gives way to particular history in Genesis 12, God's story gets much more personal. He chooses a single man named Abraham, makes a covenant with him, and begins to separate people for Himself. This relationship, as well as all relationships with God that follow, becomes the stage for revealing what God is like. Through Abraham, God shows us what it means to hear and know Him, implying that this kind of closeness is open to anyone who seeks it. The patriarchs are clear evidence that God designed human beings for relationship; Abraham becomes a case study in how to become God's friend.

But it's an odd friendship at first. Abraham's story begins with his wife's barrenness and his family's wandering. These are cold contradictions to the original design—fruitfulness and a garden to live in—but they make a perfect environment for a God who wants to restore His people to their design by making promises about descendants and land. How better to show His purposes and power than to take a man with no children and promise innumerable offspring, or to call a drifting nomad into a land to be passed on from generation to generation? God delights in turning contradictions into miraculous fulfillments of His plan.

This is how God works, as we discover throughout history— biblical history and our own personal stories. He steps into our crises and makes them the platform for His displays of character and power. We have needs, He makes promises, and then He fulfills them—sometimes after long and excruciating delays in which our faith stretches and strengthens. Growing in faith and in our relationships with God is a process, and rarely a comfortable one.

If we learn anything from the patriarchs in Genesis, it's that being chosen by God is full of both *pain* and *promise*.

For Abraham and Sarah, the interplay between pain and promise lasts for the twenty-five years they wait for a son, with lots of questions and missteps along the way—Abraham fails to defend his wife, fathers a son with Sarah's servant, doesn't exactly honor the biological mother of that first child, suggests alternative solutions to God's promise, and laughs when the promise is reaffirmed. Nevertheless, the New Testament commends his faith and tells us he did not waver. When the child of the promise is a young man, Abraham's belief in God's faithfulness must endure the ultimate test—a sacrifice of the only visible means for the promises to be fulfilled: his son Isaac. God appears at times in Abraham's story to be a cruel tease—a promiser who doesn't follow through or a giver who takes His gifts back—yet He makes it clear that He rewards those who believe Him persistently and in spite of appearances. He looks for those who insist on trusting Him even when His will seems to make no sense. Though God certainly knows the story He is writing, Abraham cannot understand the significance of the drama as he offers Isaac—the graphic picture of a Father offering His Son as a sacrifice on a cross centuries later. Still, Abraham's faith has grown to the point of implicit obedience, the kind of obedience that we admire in retrospect but would have condemned in the moment. Surely, a man of faith would realize that God's voice would never order such a brutal act. But it *is* God's voice, and Abraham complies. He sees beyond the visible. Eternal kingdoms are built on such faith.

Sarah, too, is later commended in Scripture for her faith, even though she has as many struggles with the promise as Abraham does. Like Abraham, she laughs at the promise when it's resurrected after years of waiting and then denies to God Himself that she laughed. God's response—"Is anything too hard for the Lord?"—becomes a foundational issue for all people of faith. Of course nothing is too hard for Him. He can meet the needs of a servant named Hagar as she tries to survive exile in the desert with Abraham's "plan B" son. He can protect Sarah even when Abraham doesn't. He can work our worst mistakes into His plans. He can judge rebellious cities such as Sodom and Gomorrah and still show grace in the midst of the judgment. He sets Himself up for miracles to come—in the formation of the Jewish nation, in the centuries of preparation for the coming of the Messiah, and in our lives today.

Is anything too hard for God? This is the issue we all must settle in our hearts. Are we willing to trust God's promises and wait for Him to fulfill them? God's story with His people begins with hope, promises, and faith and continues with those same themes today. Even now, we experience the hope of His promises to the degree that we embrace them.

## Questions for Reflection

In what ways do you relate to Abraham and Sarah's long wait for a fulfilled promise? What temptations did they face in the process? What similar temptations have you faced, and how have you overcome them?

 DAY 5

# GENESIS 25–36

We see the pain and promise of being chosen not only in Abraham but also in his grandson Jacob. Jacob wrestles with God one night—or for most of his life, depending on how we read his story—and lives to tell about it. In fact, he prevails against God, persevering to the point that the divine wrestler "s[ees] that he could not overpower him" (Genesis 32:25, NIV). That merits not a rebuke, as our religious instincts would expect, but an honorable name change and the founding of a nation by that name. God births Israel in that encounter. This God of relationship apparently invites wrestling from those made in His image and lowers Himself into a genuine give-and-take connection with them. It's true that He requires faith, but He also provokes questions and honors those bold enough to struggle with Him. A God who created people simply for a master/servant relationship would never tolerate such a thing. A God who created people for intimacy would. That's the kind of God we see from the earliest pages of Scripture.

Jacob's story begins the same way his grandparents' story began—with barrenness. His mother, Rebekah, can't conceive. For some reason, barrenness is a significant theme in Scripture. God gave Sarah, Rebekah, Rachel, Hannah, Elizabeth, and other women the children they desired, but only after many long, painful years of waiting. It's a picture of the circumstances we all face, whether for ourselves (the dreams and desires we long to have fulfilled), for our families and churches (the mission and purpose God has given us), or for our world (the redemption of this broken, groaning creation). God is a master of bringing hope out of hopelessness, fruitfulness out of barrenness, fulfillment out of impossibilities, and even life out of death. Eventually, Isaac and Rebekah are blessed with twins, who seem to battle for primacy even before birth. Esau is born first, but barely, with Jacob grabbing his brother's heel on the way out of the womb.

The competition continues for years. Jacob finagles the birthright from his slightly older brother, who gives it up far too willingly. When the time comes for Isaac to give his sons the family blessing, Jacob and his mother deceive Isaac into giving Jacob the blessing intended for Esau. This leads to Jacob's flight—ostensibly to find a wife from the old "home" country, but really to rescue his life from the violent tendencies of his enraged brother. It is in the midst of such uncertainty, passion, conflict, and guilt that Jacob encounters God. He has a dream, a nighttime vision of a stairway between heaven and earth with angels going up and down. Above this stairway, God Himself reiterates Abraham's covenant to Jacob, the one who will now carry it forward. To Jacob, the place of meeting had just been a place to lay his head for the night. But God was there. Jacob names the place *Bethel*, which means "the house of God," and God's holy presence there prompts a very conditional vow: *If* God will protect Jacob and bring him safely back to the land one day, then Jacob will be loyal to God. As tentative as this promise is, it's the first significant step on an even more momentous spiritual journey that will shape salvation history forever.

That's what significant spiritual steps do. They shape history. Jacob could not have known that journey would lead to the love of his life, a bride named Rachel, and that marrying her would bring him face-to-face with the same kind of deception he had inflicted on his father. His mother's brother, who was also becoming his father-in-law, switched brides before the ceremony, and in a culture in which women often remained veiled, Jacob didn't realize until morning that he had married Rachel's sister, Leah. He also could not have known that this injustice, which resulted in his having two wives—he married Rachel the next week after agreeing to another seven years of labor—would lead to twelve sons who would form the identity of the nation of Israel, the name given to Jacob after his wrestling match with God. At times, his personal life was a mess. But his journey had an everlasting purpose.

Through enormous family dysfunction—we read of rape and retribution and hostile rivalries—God shapes the story for His purposes. We don't know how He does that, but it's extremely comforting because we all, to some degree, have dysfunctional families. If God can speak into the chaos of the patriarchal family and bring meaningful design, just as He spoke into the chaos of

Genesis and brought forth a world teeming with life and beauty, He can speak into our lives with the same purpose and the same result. Even a life filled with missteps and mistakes can be a vital part of God's plan.

## QUESTIONS FOR REFLECTION

In what ways do you relate to Jacob's wrestling match with God? Why do you think God invites us to interact with Him like that? In what ways does it encourage you that God's chosen people in Genesis were at times examples of extreme dysfunction? How does this challenge modern perceptions of the kinds of people God chooses to work through?

 DAY 6

# GENESIS 37–50

Joseph, Jacob's eleventh son and also his favorite, is one of the few people in Scripture with a sterling reputation throughout his story, yet he endures some of the most difficult circumstances of any biblical character. He has God-given dreams that offend everyone around him, as God-given dreams often do. He's betrayed by his own family, sold into slavery, slandered into an unjust prison sentence, and seemingly forgotten in captivity—and God lets it all unfold without stepping in to vindicate him. Joseph is left to wonder whether God is really good and in charge. For some time, God keeps him in limbo, and we are given no glimpses of the questions Joseph must have had.

But God continues to favor him, even in oppressive circumstances, and He vindicates him in the end. Joseph gets revelation from God that provides a practical solution for real-life society—Egypt's society, in fact. This region-wide blessing of provision reveals that God's interest in and love for nations extends well beyond Israel. Joseph comes through this lengthy, painful process with grand statements of God's sovereignty over even the worst evils and human errors.

As with Abraham and Isaac, God uses Joseph to paint a dramatic picture of another descendant of Jacob's, who would come centuries later. This favored Son would also make extravagant but offensive claims that would provoke violent reactions from many of Jacob's offspring. He would be considered dead by the family of Israel, but later found to be alive. In the meantime, He would become a blessing to Gentiles and eventually be recognized by the tribes of Jacob. For all eternity, He would faithfully represent God's goodness and express God's revelation for everyone to see.

We see ourselves in the characters of Scripture—many besides Abraham, Jacob, and Joseph, but especially these three. We relate to their struggles of faith, their problems and pain, and perhaps even the enormous dysfunction of their families. We take comfort in the fact that God works through people like these. We look to them as examples of how to hold on to promises; how to follow God without knowing where we're going; how to cling to the belief that God is good even when circumstances suggest otherwise; how to surrender to God's will when He makes it clear; and how to wrestle with His will when He doesn't. These stories become epic, life-altering sagas for us.

In Genesis, God crafts thousands of years of real-life experiences that display who He is and what He intends for His people. Genesis contains a wealth of spiritual truths and fascinating pictures of the coming Messiah—the One who will crush the serpent's head, who appears to Abraham as a mysterious priest of peace and righteousness named Melchizedek, who submits to His Father's sacrificial offering like Isaac did, and who is betrayed by His brothers and will reconcile with them after He blesses other nations. At its most fundamental level, Genesis teaches us that God is zealous for His broken creation, that He desires a relationship with His people, and that the condition for that relationship is, above all else, faith.

When life gets tough, we need to remember that pain and hardship can be explained by the debacle in Eden. But the story doesn't end there, though many people act as if it does. Genesis tells us that history and our own lives are going somewhere and that faith is the key to getting in on the plan. Yes, we have to wrestle with the serpent's question every day: *Is God really good?* We don't deal with temptations about eating from the wrong tree, at least not literally. But the temptation to doubt God replays again and again in our daily lives. We ask God whether He is holding out on us or not, whether He's looking out for us or we're left to look out for ourselves. And we should know the answers to those questions. When in doubt, we can look to Abraham, Jacob, Joseph, and the other faith figures in Genesis for examples of how to apply those answers to our lives. They prove it: Yes, God is good. No, He isn't holding out on us. Yes, He's in charge and working all things together for good. And yes, there's a plan. And it's only just beginning.

## QUESTIONS FOR REFLECTION

In what ways do you relate to Joseph's trials? How do you respond to being treated unfairly? How easily do you express forgiveness? How does knowing that God is ultimately in charge of your life make it easier to forgive others and trust Him in the midst of difficult circumstances?

DAY 7

# EXODUS 1–15

Genesis ends with Joseph in a position of authority in Egypt, the entire family of Jacob safe and secure with Joseph, and a clear picture of a God who guides and provides and defends His people. Some four centuries later, as the book of Exodus opens, the picture has changed dramatically. Where is the God who relentlessly seeks a relationship with His people, who pursues them and draws them into His presence, who guides, provides, and defends? The people of God are now slaves, harshly oppressed in the same country where God once led them in order to provide for them. Over time, the place of blessing has become a place of captivity. The former wanderers are tied down.

Life with God often involves such contradictions. We live long stretches of time between promise and fulfillment, and what we choose to believe about God during those times shapes our experience with Him. Like Israel, we cry out to Him for deliverance. And, as with Israel, God hears. He may not respond as quickly as we want Him to—Israel wasn't delivered until some eighty years after a brutal pharaoh had tried to extinguish a generation of Hebrew males—but God does hear and He does respond. Faith compels us to persevere until He does.

When the time comes for God to deliver Israel, He uses someone to lead the way who himself has been delivered. As a child, Moses survived the extermination of Hebrew males because his parents floated him in the Nile River and because he was then discovered and raised by Pharaoh's daughter. He learned the ways of Egypt but identified with his own people—to the point that he fled into exile at the age of forty after trying to defend them in his own strength. Forty years later, God encounters him in the form of a burning bush, calls him against his objections to return to the courts of the reigning pharaoh—possibly someone he had grown up with and who would remember the reasons for his exile. It's an absurd plan, a seeming suicide mission—Moses' protests aren't unfounded, at least on the surface—and yet it comes with divine guarantees. God wants to free His people. Why? So they can worship Him freely.

The first part of Exodus is familiar to many because it makes for entertaining Sunday school lessons and dramatic movies. God methodically executes a series of ten plagues to convince Pharaoh to let His people go, each one an affront to the power of Egypt's gods and an affirmation of God's own power as the one true God—the "I Am Who I Am." The last of the plagues is particularly harsh, but necessarily so; the captors of God's people don't give up their claims easily. But the death of Egypt's firstborn sons in this plague secures Israel's freedom, just as the death of God's only Son would one day secure the freedom of all who believe. Both events involve a covenant of blood. Apparently, God's rescues are often traumatic. His pursuit of a relationship with His people costs a lot.

The climax of this deliverance is the miraculous escape through the Red Sea. After Pharaoh changes his mind and pursues the newly freed captives, God leads them to an exceedingly vulnerable position at the edge of the sea. It looks like disaster. Why would this good God, who has promised deliverance—and to this point has miraculously obtained it—put His people in such a difficult spot? We ask that question often because we find ourselves in similar situations. We follow God and somehow land in predicaments, and like Israel, we mutter complaints about the guidance (or lack of guidance) we've received. We scarcely realize the deliverance God has planned. Even when it seems a long time coming, we can know there's glory in His victories, however they come.

The victory in Exodus—a certain slaughter averted by a deliverance so thorough that the enemy is destroyed in the process—becomes the defining moment in Israel's history. Hundreds of years after Israel passed between the parted waters and Egypt's army drowned when the gap disappeared, psalms would celebrate the power God demonstrated on that day. God, who had seemed absent for four centuries, shows Himself in a way that will be remembered and celebrated forever. The Egyptian captivity and the Exodus show us that God's works can be both slow and sudden. They take years to develop and are executed in a moment. That may frustrate us at times, but it always gives us reason to hope.

## QUESTIONS FOR REFLECTION

What does the Exodus show us about God's nature? What aspects of His nature did Israel experience? What aspects of God's nature do you experience when you're in need?

DAY 8

# EXODUS 16–34

The deliverance through the Red Sea seems like the end of Israel's troubles, but as most people can testify, spiritual victories are rarely followed by comfort and peace. The people find themselves in a wasteland without food and water—though God provides both, it's not before He has endured some unacceptable complaining from them—and then under attack from the Amalekites. The great deliverance is still a work in progress, and the people forget far too easily that God is on their side, even after witnessing numerous miracles. The Provider and Protector is still at work, and the people can see Him only if they will stop griping long enough to notice.

On the safe side of the sea, God leads His people to a mountain and reveals Himself more clearly. The events at Sinai are both awe inspiring and terrifying: a three-day preparation and cleansing period, a dense cloud, thunder and lightning, a loud horn blast from heaven, smoke and fire, a voice from above, strict boundaries around the sacred space, and a threat of death for anyone who gets too close. These events are also a tangible endorsement of the instructions about to be handed down through Moses: the Ten Commandments and numerous accompanying laws.

First and foremost are laws about worship. As always, God's desire is to be known, loved, and appreciated. "No other gods" are not the words of a demanding dictator; they are the words of a God who declares His name to be *Jealous*. It's a mind-boggling but scriptural fact: The infinite God of the universe is intensely jealous for the affection of human hearts. His commandments are driven by love.

Centuries of rabbinic teaching have treated the Sinai encounter as a betrothal ceremony. In fact, it was considered so by the prophets (Jeremiah 2:2; Ezekiel 16:8), who often called Israel's unfaithfulness *adultery*. Betrothal ceremonies in Israel were later patterned after this event—a trumpet blast, a bride price, the terms of the betrothal contract specifically stated. God never intended for the commandments to be a religious formula, but rather a marriage agreement. Though God has already proven His sovereignty and lordship, He desires a deeper relationship. Never mind that the people at the foot of the mountain get restless and betray God by worshiping an idol while Moses is on the mountain receiving the commandments. The eternal God is persistent. Though these people who have been delivered specifically for the purpose of worshiping God will often fail at their task, the implications of their relationship with Him will play out through the rest of Scripture, even to the final chapter. Sinai is a major step toward restoring the intimacy lost in the Garden of Eden.

But even as God implements this betrothal agreement, Aaron

and the people of Israel are at the bottom of the mountain giving their worship to a false god. The golden calf episode seems to threaten this new covenant; adultery is never a good thing, and certainly not immediately after the engagement. God threatens to destroy the people, and Moses becomes a model of intercession, putting himself in the line of God's wrath along with the people. God relents.

Then Moses seems to grow even bolder. He refuses to lead the people into the Promised Land unless God personally goes with them, making His presence manifest along the way. Moses wants to see that presence. Though he has already seen a burning bush, witnessed the power of numerous miracles and plagues, walked between walls of water, and stood in the cloud of glory and lightning and fire on Sinai, he now asks to see God's glory. He knows there is more than what he has already encountered, some glimpse more personal and powerful than the drama of recent events. And God complies. Not completely—no one can see the face of God and live (though Scripture has already declared that God speaks to Moses face-to-face, as to a friend)—but God at least passes by Moses, declares His name and nature, and gives Moses a glimpse of Himself. This brush with deity reveals God's heart—compassionate, gracious, slow to anger, loving and faithful, yet still relentlessly righteous—and causes Moses' face to radiate with glory. This heightened intensity further establishes God's presence among His people.

God, who has just threatened to destroy His people, has instead been swayed by someone who stands between His righteousness and the people's rebellion. This dynamic will become a central theme of the relationship between the Creator and His broken creation.

Moses has to plead for Israel's forgiveness often. His verbal exchanges with God throughout this season of Israel's history don't show us a God who is ready to snap whenever His people disobey, as some people seem to think. No, they show us a God who confronts His people with the divine distance that rightfully should be observed among the fallen, and then practically invites them to step in with hearts that cry out for mercy, that desire His presence above protocol, and that would rather forfeit the plan than accept the gifts without the Giver. In other words, God is pleased when we seek personal encounters with Him rather than simply offering Him right behavior. And He meets us when we do. Those who, like Moses, risk offending Him by saying, "I want all of You or none of You," find that they haven't offended Him at all. Their audacity connects with His heart and provokes the gift He wanted to give all along: Himself.

## QUESTIONS FOR REFLECTION

Why do you think the Israelites struggled with faith even after seeing dramatic miracles such as the ten plagues and the parting of the Red Sea? How did God feel about their complaints in the wilderness? In what ways are you tempted to complain about the ways God deals with you?

 DAY 9

# EXODUS 35–40

Just as the Ten Commandments are a relational agreement that will help bring God's people back in line with His heart and restore the intimacy between God and humanity that was lost in Eden, so are the instructions that come in the aftermath. God gives Moses an extraordinarily detailed design for a Tabernacle—a place to meet with Him. Every inch of this meeting place is sacred, but especially the Holy of Holies, where the Ark of the Covenant and

God's presence will dwell. God will express His desire to be present with His people even more deeply later in Scripture, but this tent of meeting is a step in that direction. He makes it clear that He wants to bridge the gap between Himself and fallen humanity. Closeness is very important to Him.

God also gives detailed instructions for seven highly symbolic feasts. Like Genesis, Exodus contains numerous veiled references to the future Messiah. The Passover is a graphic picture of the sacrifice of Jesus—in fact, the entire Exodus event is a remarkable portrait of salvation in its fullness—but all of the feasts tell a story that will only make sense centuries after they are first described. The Festival of Weeks (Pentecost) points to a future outpouring of God's Spirit—the Law written on human hearts—and the fall feasts point to an atonement, a future day of judgment, and a regathering of God's people from the ends of the earth. The richness of the symbolism in these feasts shows that the story of God's people has divine origins. It also confirms that God has had a plan from the beginning. Though some people see a demanding deity in these pages, a careful reader will see a portrait of an artist—a God to whom colors and scents and proportions are vitally important, a God who is painting a stunning picture of His purposes before they ever play out. This is not the story of a religion in the making; it's the story of a God on a mission to be known.

Though several well-known events in Exodus represent climaxes in the story—the Passover, the Red Sea crossing, and the giving of the Ten Commandments, for example—the spiritual peaks of this book often go unnoticed. First, God delivers Israel not just for the sake of deliverance but so they might worship Him freely, openly, and distinctly. Second, the betrothal theme of Sinai shapes Israel's identity even today and adds depth to many of Jesus' parables and other "bride of Christ" references in the New Testament. And one of the most significant events of Scripture often gets neglected by the drama of the story—namely,

Moses' plea to see God's glory. The "I Am" who called to Moses from a burning bush now describes His nature to Moses on Mount Sinai—and the description is nothing like that of gods worshiped by other nations at that time. God declares who He is: "The God of compassion and mercy! I am slow to anger and filled with unfailing love and faithfulness. I lavish unfailing love to a thousand generations. I forgive iniquity, rebellion, and sin" (Exodus 34:6-7).

God's love extends to thousands of generations, while His punishment extends to only three or four. He is just, but He chooses mercy. His holiness is dangerous, but His presence is still made available to those who seek Him. He chooses to overcome a lot in order to be known.

When reading Exodus, many people only see a God who requires obedience and prescribes painfully obscure rituals. This view misses the heart of God completely. In lives both then and now, He desires uncompromising love; He chooses to be present and available; He shows Himself to be both strong and compassionate; He pursues relationships, even in the face of our unfaithfulness; and He guides anyone who is sensitive enough to follow His personal leading—whether by visible cloud and fire or by inner promptings of His Spirit—rather than formulaic principles. He is majestic, powerful, and uncompromising, but even His strictest commandments flow from His desire for exclusive love. His highest priority for us is not our ability to do things for Him, but our capacity to know and love Him. After all, He created the world; He can do things for Himself. His goal is to relate to others. He wants hearts.

That's why the story of the Exodus begins with "so they can worship me" and ends with instructions on how to recognize God's presence and follow His lead by watching the cloud by day and the fire by night. This book is a story of personal encounters. God sets us free so we can freely experience Him.

## Questions for Reflection

How did the Israelites respond to God's presence? In what ways do you think God wants to make His presence known in your life? Why do you think God's guidance of Israel (a cloud by day and a pillar of fire by night that could move at any time) was unpredictable? What does that tell us about how He leads us?

 DAY 10

# LEVITICUS

Leviticus can be a confusing and intimidating book, but one theme comes through clearly: "You must be holy because I, the LORD your God, am holy" (Leviticus 19:2). In other words, people called into relationship with God are meant to connect with Him and become like Him. There are personal and corporate implications for calling Him "the LORD your God." This is not a *casual* relationship.

But what does "holy" mean? Most modern Christians equate holiness with righteousness or even religiosity. We often define it in terms of what we don't do or what we stand against rather than what we are called to do and stand for. But thinking of holiness simply as purity or righteousness is a dreadful misperception. The word really means to be "set apart," to have a sacred purpose, and to be so dedicated to that purpose that we separate ourselves from anything that distracts us from it. Holiness certainly includes righteousness, but that's only because we separate ourselves from rebellion against God and become like Him, and because He is righteous and pure. If He were a mean-spirited or vindictive God, holiness would involve separating ourselves from anything that wasn't mean-spirited or vindictive and taking on that character. But because God is relentlessly, passionately, and unfathomably *good*, holiness for us means becoming relentlessly, passionately, and unfathomably good. At its core, holiness means *turning away* from anything—thought, word, or deed—that contradicts our relationship with God and *embracing* our relationship with Him in every area of life.

Since the Ten Commandments have been given and the Tabernacle built, the book of Leviticus is filled with elaborate and complex instructions that define holiness in the religious lives, community lives, and personal lives of God's people. The book is primarily directed at priests—that is, the tribe of Levi, to whom God gave the task of maintaining Israel's worship—who need to know how to give visible expression to Israel's relationship with an invisible God.

The purpose of the Tabernacle was to host God's presence, and nearly everything in Leviticus relates to that purpose. From our perspective, we tend to see the first sixteen chapters as relating to Israel's ritual practices and the last ten chapters as relating to the people's ethical behavior; however, that distinction was not nearly as strong in the minds of the Israelites. For them, the sacredness of God's presence encompassed *all* of life—the whole person, individually, socially, ethically, morally, and in whatever other terms we can frame our existence.

For an ancient culture, that all-of-life approach involved practices that seem archaic to us today. We get strong impressions of blood flowing continuously from altars on account of sin; of the "otherness" of a God who can't be encountered casually; of symbols and signs that must be shadows of something extraordinary in heaven. Many details for measurements and types of offerings and celebrations of feasts must point dramatically to a redemption plan and an eternal kingdom. They are pictures of a coming Messiah and an ultimate sacrifice that takes away sin, of an eternal

High Priest who intercedes for His people, and of a heavenly existence where God is worshiped and experienced openly and visibly. Yes, many of the laws protect Israel from health issues that a pre-scientific culture could not understand, but Leviticus is so much more than a hygiene manual. It is filled with imagery of spiritual realities. The prophetic acts of sacrifice, offering, personal and corporate consecration, and celebration point participants toward a future, true atonement and redemption by a merciful God who loves to be with His people. In that sense, Leviticus is a book that is better absorbed than deciphered.

When we learn to view Leviticus as an invitation into a relationship rather than as an ancient and demanding spiritual gauntlet for approaching God, it takes on much more meaning. We still may not grasp all the nuances of its rituals and ethics, but we get a strong picture of the costliness of sin and the otherness of God. And when we accept the invitation to relationship through the Messiah, who fulfills all the requirements of the Law, those pictures need to remain with us. He has paid the cost and invited us into the otherness. The shadows of eternal realities have given way to the full experience.

## QUESTIONS FOR REFLECTION

What relevance does Leviticus have for us today? What do the details about worship and purity tell us about what God desires for His people?

DAY 11

# NUMBERS 1–10

Numbers isn't a very attractive portion of Scripture to the casual reader. Its name can take some of the blame for that, as can the fact that it begins with a census (hence the name). But contrary to initial appearances, this book isn't just lists of names and numbers. It's the story of life in the wilderness—a story every single one of us can relate to. We're all somewhere between a promise of God and its fulfillment, and the journey isn't always easy. We face hardships, wrestle with questions, complain from time to time, and wonder if we will ever get to where we're going. In other words, we're a lot like the Israelites on the way to the Promised Land.

As the book opens, God tells Moses to take a census—a record of all the men of fighting age. Centuries later, David would be harshly punished for taking a military census, presumably because it revealed his reliance on human strength rather than God's. But in this case, God is the one ordering the count, and the result serves not only as an indication of the size of Israel's army, but also as a testimony of how many Jews—real, flesh-and-blood people with names and personal histories—were delivered from Egypt. This is no small clan of Jacob's descendants wandering through the desert. It is the makings of a nation.

As in many other portions of the Torah, the first five books of Hebrew Scripture, much is made of keeping the community pure—from disease, from immorality, from casual or halfhearted worship. Even with its strange laws—such as the test to determine whether a woman has committed adultery—one gets the impression that the calling of the community to be "set apart" is far more important than the interests of each individual. These are God's people, after all, the ones through whom He will continue to reveal

Himself, the nation designated to serve as a priest to other nations. It has to be distinct in all ways—culturally, morally, ethically, ritually, and socially. The people cannot merely blend in with the Middle Eastern landscape.

Instructions are given for sacred vows, such as those of a Nazirite, a person who becomes especially separated to the Lord for a designated period of time. The priests are given special words to use to bless the nation and call upon God's favor for each of its members. This blessing essentially puts God's name on the Israelites and causes His face to shine on them. Special sacrifices are offered to consecrate the Tabernacle and its articles of worship in order to maintain the nation's unique relationship with God. In order for God's presence to be realized, the right environment must be cultivated.

This principle applies not only to ancient Israel's wilderness years, but also to our own lives. Between our deliverance from captivity and our full experience of the Promised Land of heaven, we won't get to know God very well if we aren't careful about our calling. He calls us to pursue Him passionately—like a newly freed people, like a Nazirite who vows wholehearted dedication, like a nation unwilling to blend in with its surroundings or settle for status quo. He calls us to worship sacrificially, with genuine offerings of heart, mind, and spirit—and even with material possessions. As we do, He establishes our identity completely in Him.

God knows this journey will involve battles, require unity and dedication, and be centered on worship. In Leviticus, He designates trumpet blasts (on special silver trumpets) for all three of these aspects, committing Himself to step in and fight alongside His people, unite them, and celebrate with them. It is significant that the Ark of the Covenant—the symbol of God's holy presence—leads the way on this journey through the wilderness, and that the tribe of Judah, whose name comes from the word for praise, follows first. Every detail prescribed by God through Moses points toward something about God's personality, His ways, or His mission. And every faithful step along the way brings His people closer to their destination—and to Him.

## QUESTIONS FOR REFLECTION

In what ways are we living between our deliverance and our Promised Land? What aspects of the wilderness experience can you relate to?

 DAY 12

# NUMBERS 11–36

One might think that following such clear evidence of God's presence as a cloud of glory or a pillar of fire—through parted seas and beyond hostile armies, no less—would cultivate a sense of security, but the Israelites are still restless enough to wonder whether God is going to come through. Numbers is filled with a repeated cycle of complaining that at times develops into outright rebellion against Moses' leadership—and ultimately God's as well. The people are tired of manna, so God gives them enough quail to make them wish they had never asked. Miriam and Aaron are tired of their brother, Moses, and contemptuous of his wife, so God rebukes them and explains why His relationship with Moses is unique and not subject to popular vote. A rebellion led by a priest prompts God's fury to the point that some of the rebels are swallowed by the ground and others are burned by His fire. Desert life isn't easy; the pain of Egypt is forgotten and its pleasures remembered far too well. Many of the Israelites want to go back.

The most significant episode of complaining and rebellion

occurs after Moses sends twelve spies into the Promised Land. The purpose of this mission was to scout the land, not determine whether it could be taken. All the spies were impressed with the fruitfulness of the land, but ten were intimidated by the size of its people and the fortifications of its cities. Only two, Caleb and Joshua, remembered that the Promised Land was actually the *promised* land. They saw the size of the inhabitants but were more impressed with the size of their God. When the spies come back with conflicting reports, the people are swayed by the negative perspective of the majority. They cry out in desperation, certain that Moses and God have led them into the wilderness to die. Moses intercedes for them—a frequent event in the wilderness, a picture of Jesus' ministry, and an example for us to follow—so God forgives; but He doesn't overlook their lack of faith. He will wait for this generation to die in the wilderness and bring the next generation into the land. Of the adult generation at the time of the Exodus, only Joshua and Caleb will live long enough to inherit the promise. Everyone else will die.

Clearly, this is a devastating consequence, a dramatic example of how God feels about negative expectations and mistrust of His goodness. He sees it as contempt (Numbers 14:11). Centuries later, the writer of Hebrews will call it "an evil heart of unbelief" (Hebrews 3:12, NKJV), reminding his readers that God's promises are inherited through both faith and endurance (Hebrews 6:12). Because the vast majority of Israelites in the wilderness have neither faith nor endurance, they miss out on God's plan for them.

Israel's complaints and rebellions bring plenty of negative consequences. Many people die under the hand of God's judgment, Miriam suffers from leprosy for a short time, and Moses himself is disqualified from entering the land when he and Aaron react in anger and presumption by striking a rock for water to flow miraculously from it. But there are some good consequences, too. After hearing one particular round of complaints, God tells Moses to select seventy elders to help him handle the administration of the nation—a model for later Jewish government in councils such as the Sanhedrin. After the rebellion led by Korah the priest, God reaffirms Aaron's priesthood by causing his staff to blossom. And after God responds to a later incident of bitter grumbling and impatience by sending venomous snakes, the only remedy is for Moses to hold up a bronze serpent (a representation of the curse) and have the people gaze at it for protection. Jesus will draw a parallel between this remedy and His cross in John 3. Like the Passover, the bronze serpent serves as a powerful image of how God rescues His people from their fallenness.

After the twelve spies give their reports, the people are turned away from the land and continue to wander in the wilderness. Along the way, there are victories in battle, Miriam and Aaron die and are buried, and an Amorite king hires a prophet named Balaam to curse Israel. After contending with a donkey and an angel on the way, the prophet's words come out as blessing, infuriating his patron king. So Balaam counsels Amorite women to seduce Israel's men—perhaps corrupting God's people will be more effective than cursing them. The result is an ugly episode of adultery and idolatry, with overtones similar to the golden calf incident at the base of Mount Sinai.

By the end of this diverse book, God commissions Joshua as Moses' successor and gives instructions for taking the land. The winding path toward the Promised Land is reflected by the circuitous nature of the story, with all its examples of obstacles, setbacks, and distractions, as well as hopes and expectations for the future. The journey continues on; the cloud and fire still lead; the Land of Promise still waits to be conquered.

We see throughout Numbers that the distance between promise and fulfillment has more to do with character and faith than with miles and years. God is intensely interested not only in getting us into our Land of Promise, but also in how we handle the journey. In fact, He is more than willing for that journey to take a while if we aren't ready. And He will do whatever it takes to prepare us.

## QUESTIONS FOR REFLECTION

Why do you think God reacted so harshly to the Israelites' complaints? Why did their lack of faith cause a generation to miss out on something God had promised?

 DAY 13

# DEUTERONOMY

Jesus quoted Scripture often, and the book He quoted most often was not Genesis, the Psalms, or one of the Prophets, but Deuteronomy. Perhaps that's because Deuteronomy serves as a profound, interpretive summary of the books preceding it and as Israel's foundational story. Addressed to the next generation, now poised to enter the Promised Land, Deuteronomy reiterates the events after the Exodus and the laws given to the previous generation, which has, for the most part, died in the wilderness. Constructed around three speeches by Moses, Deuteronomy reviews the story of the deliverance from Egypt and the journey through the Red Sea to Sinai and through the wilderness and recaps the laws and feasts and priestly practices instructed by God through Moses. In many ways, it's a pivotal book between Israel's foundations and its future.

The book opens forty years into a journey that could have taken only a few short weeks, with the children of the rebellious generation still east of the Jordan River, outside the land of

Canaan. Moses recounts the history of the journey from Horeb (Mount Sinai), reminding the people of the faithlessness and complaining that has kept them from fulfillment for so long. It must be hard hearing such critical words about their parents, but this generation needs to know of all the stubbornness and idolatrous ways of the past because such attitudes will not be appropriate in the Land of Promise. Perhaps Moses' strongest theme throughout his messages is this: *God alone is worthy of worship.* As a nation that showcases who God is, the Israelites are called to serve Him alone. These are the words of a treaty, with terms and conditions clearly spelled out. If the people want to live long in the land, they must be faithful.

Perhaps the best-known passage in Deuteronomy is the *Shema* (Deuteronomy 6:4)—the statement of faith that makes monotheism a nonnegotiable truth among God's people—and the follow-up command that Jesus and other rabbis will later designate as the greatest commandment (Deuteronomy 6:5). In other words, there's only one God, and He wants our wholehearted love. This is the key to understanding our existence. In two short sentences, we're told emphatically who created us and why. In the midst of these books of the Law, which list God's instructions in often-tedious detail, the greater and deeper commandment is purely relational. God's highest goal for us isn't our obedience, our service, our testimony for Him, or any other behavioral outcome. It's that we adore Him. Yes, love has implications in all other areas, but first and foremost, our relationship with God is a matter of the heart. If we don't love Him fully, we're missing our purpose.

That speaks volumes about God. He created human beings in His image, not to have more servants—the hosts of heaven serve Him rather well already—but to be known by fully sentient beings who can appreciate Him for who He is. We have the capacity to experience God's love, compassion, mercy, tenderness, majesty, power, jealousy, righteousness, justice, humility, and all other aspects of His glory. According to the inspired words of Moses, and later of Jesus, that is to be the focus of our lives.

But this God who desires our love also wants us to display His character, so Deuteronomy and the other books of the Law are filled with standards. In Deuteronomy 28, God lays out the results of being in relationship with Him. If the people live consistent with His character by keeping His Word, they will be blessed extravagantly. Their prosperity and favor in the land will never cease. But if they forsake Him, falling into idolatry and rebelling against His ways, they will be cursed. The enormous privilege of having a relationship with God will turn into an enormous burden, and they will be cast from the land.

These blessings and curses in Deuteronomy explain much of the rest of the Old Testament—why God disciplines and judges His people, why the prophets warn about a coming exile, and why the people experience success or failure in their dealings with each other and with other nations. The covenant is a blessing when it is kept and a huge crisis when it isn't. As we will see, it turns out to be a crisis throughout much of Israel's history.

Deuteronomy ends with the commissioning of Joshua to lead the people into the Promised Land, Moses utters his final words and prophecies (which include the famous and strongly worded "Song of Moses") and dies on Mount Nebo. All of the Exodus leaders—Miriam, Aaron, and now Moses—have died, perhaps as a symbolic and divine statement that this law and priesthood will not truly be able to get God's people into their Land of Promise. But a man bearing the name of Joshua—the same name as a Savior who will come centuries later—will.

## QUESTIONS FOR REFLECTION

What is God's primary purpose for us? What are the obligations of being in this kind of relationship? What are the benefits?

DAY 14

# JOSHUA

The book of Joshua is about taking territory. It has obvious, literal meaning for its time, but also many spiritual parallels for ours. God has called each of us to enter into His promise, receive an inheritance as coheirs with His Son, and help shape His Kingdom by working for Him and allowing Him to work through us. Along the way, we will need to be strong and courageous, adhere unwaveringly to God's ways, avoid compromise and unhealthy alliances, and persevere through trials and long battles. We see all of these lessons in the historical parable of the conquest of Canaan. It's a template for how we enter God's promises.

It's significant, then, that the book begins with God Himself repeatedly encouraging Joshua to be strong and courageous and to immerse himself in God's Word. These are vital keys to living a Kingdom lifestyle. Other keys follow: a time of consecration (this generation of Israelites had not been circumcised), a strange encounter with God's presence (the angel identifies himself only as the commander of God's armies), a hard lesson in obedience (one man keeps some of Jericho's plunder for himself and causes the nation to lose its next battle), a hard lesson in compromise (the leaders are duped into a treaty with locals that limits their choices in the future), and so on. By following God's instructions, the people are able to put the past behind them and press on into the promise—albeit with stumbling, at times. Their conquest is decisive, though not always thorough; many Canaanites remain in the land by the time the book ends. But God fights on behalf of His people when they trust and depend on Him, even altering physical laws to extend a day. He *will* fulfill His plans on behalf of those who believe.

This theme is reinforced in the portrayal of several characters who demonstrate great faith. Aside from Joshua himself, the first is a prostitute named Rahab, a resident of Jericho who is put in the position of choosing sides. When Joshua sends two spies to scout the land—the same number that came back with a good report forty years earlier—Rahab becomes their key contact, hiding them and helping them strategize in exchange for her life and the lives of her family members. When Israel conquers Jericho, Rahab's life is preserved and she is honored for her assistance. Centuries later, her name will appear in the genealogy of the Messiah.

Another great figure of faith is Caleb, one of the two surviving spies from the previous generation (the other is Joshua, of course). Despite his firm belief that God would overcome the giants and give His people the land He had promised, Caleb spent forty years suffering the consequences of the people's rebellion. Now in his eighties, he is still full of life and vigor and zealous to receive his piece of the promise. God has preserved Caleb's life and rewarded his faith.

Interwoven with the accounts of these two prominent characters are the stories of parted waters and generally steady conquest. God waits until the Jordan's waters are at flood stage before parting the river for His people to pass through—a revealing illustration of how He steps into our problems when the obstacles are greatest. The famous story of the battle of Jericho shows us that no obstacle is too great for God, nor any method too strange. The varied approaches to each battle show us that while God's character never changes, His methods very frequently do—evidence that we can never follow Him simply by understanding His principles, but only by having a direct relationship with Him. God's instructions to establish cities of refuge throughout the land are an early example of how His justice and compassion meet; there are penalties for wrongdoing as well as protection for suspected wrongdoers.

There is a reason God has called His people to be separate and to live in a separate land: He is in the process of revealing His nature to them through the events in their lives. The book ends with a warning that being chosen doesn't mean immunity from God's chastisement and with a challenge for the people to make a decision to serve God alone. Joshua and his household make that decision, and the people join in. They declare their undying allegiance to the Lord in the land He has given. Their future will be determined by how well they maintain their devotion.

## QUESTIONS FOR REFLECTION

What "territory" do you think God wants you to take for His Kingdom? for your family? in your work? What truths from Joshua will be most helpful as you do that?

 DAY 15

# JUDGES

The book of Joshua ends with the people vowing to put away all of their idols and serve God wholeheartedly. The book of Judges is the story of how that vow was broken again and again in succeeding generations. When we read Judges, we can't help but be incredulous at the foolishness of the nation's cycle of idolatry—how they abandon or neglect God, how God allows them to become subject to foreign oppressors, how they cry out to God in their desperation, how He raises up a leader to deliver them, how they are freed and give thanks, and how the cycle starts all over again. Then we remember that our own stories—personal, family, church, national—are just as repetitive. We cry out to God in our trouble, somehow He gets us out or brings us through, we give thanks for a brief moment, and then we get ourselves in trouble again. The cycle in Judges is all too familiar.

In the midst of all this spiritual dysfunction, we encounter some of the Bible's most colorful characters. From some, we learn more about what *not* to do rather than what we *should* do; but either way, we learn from them. The first judge, Othniel, a relative of Caleb's, becomes a deliverer because the Spirit of God is on him. The next judge, Ehud, stealthily kills Moab's leader before rallying Israel's warriors to battle. We learn from Deborah, the first judge to whom Scripture devotes significant space, that God is not reluctant to use valiant women to represent Him. We learn from Gideon that God is not reluctant to call a fearful, unassuming man a "mighty warrior" (Judges 6:12, NIV) and do extraordinary things through him—and that God prefers to receive glory for Himself than to have men usurp it through their own efforts.

As negative examples, one of Gideon's sons establishes his power through violence; a judge named Jephthah keeps a horrible vow by killing his own daughter; and a well-known judge named Samson lives out a lifelong holy vow in some very unholy ways—yet God works through him to overcome the Philistine oppressors. The book of Judges gives us the overall impression that God can accomplish His purposes through very flawed people, simply because they are chosen by Him, even if their faith is not very solid at times. Some judges become leaders almost by default; yet, despite their flaws, they do lead the people.

In many respects, the leadership vacuum we see in Judges, and all the characters that fill it, are the result of Joshua's generation failing to fully take the land. They did not completely drive out the Canaanite inhabitants. There are varying explanations for this. In Joshua 23, and at the end of Judges 2, we're told that the hostile tribes were left in the land because the Israelites have fickle, compromising hearts. The beginning of Judges 3 says it's because God wants to give the next generations experience in war. Either way, the resistance that remains within the Promised Land provides the context for Israel's relationship with God. There's a gap between the people who said they would worship Him wholeheartedly and the God who said their welfare in the land was conditional on their devotion. They need leadership, and they don't try often enough to find it in God.

Judges sets up a major historical transition found in the next section of the Bible: the kingship of Israel. The writer of this chronicle seems to lament the lack of leadership in Israel, pointing out that everyone was doing what was right in his own eyes—without regard to spiritual, moral, or cultural standards—and implying that a king was needed. Yet in 1 Samuel, we will see God Himself lamenting the nation's desire for a king, as if His leadership were not enough for them. Perhaps that's the between-the-lines message of Judges: A nation had an opportunity to be led directly by God and missed it. And though the development of a monarchy may have seemed like progress to the people, it was less than ideal in God's eyes. He desires the trust and dependence of His people, and He will lead them well if they devote themselves wholeheartedly to Him.

## Questions for Reflection

Have you seen the "Judges cycle" at work in your life? If so, how has God delivered you when you've cried out to Him? What does the book of Judges tell us about the kinds of people God works through?

DAY 16

# RUTH

Not everyone in the semi-anarchic period of the judges was law-less. A beautiful love story shows us a family and a community that lived faithfully in relationship to God. It takes place in hard times, as most good love stories do, but the hard times are overshadowed by the goodness of God, who orchestrates His favor toward those who are faithful to Him.

The story begins tragically, after a drought—one of the conse-quences of Israel's disobedience—caused a family to go searching for livelihood in neighboring Moab. This is no small gesture; it's this family's rash statement that perhaps the Promised Land isn't all that promising and maybe the rival nation's land is better. After all, plenty of people who remained in the land, including those we meet later in the story,  are enjoying a harvest by the time the fam-ily returns. But this family of four had decided to seek sustenance elsewhere, and things haven't gone well. Naomi's husband dies, and then her two sons die. She is left as a true widow with no one to take care of her but her two widowed daughters-in-law. And she is rather bitter about it.

In a sense, the book of Ruth is really the story of Naomi—of how God meets the needs of a bitter woman and restores her back into the Land of Promise and into the people of God. But along the way, it becomes the story of Ruth, a foreigner who selflessly commits to care for her mother-in-law and identify herself with God's people.

Upon returning to Bethlehem, Naomi's hometown, Ruth finds work at harvesttime in the fields of Boaz, one of Naomi's kinsmen. At Naomi's instigation, Ruth rather daringly goes into the fields at night to let Boaz know of her desire to marry him. Though no immoral behavior is implied, Israelite culture attached quite a few connotations to a single woman being out at night, sleeping in a field full of men who have been drinking, and not coming home until morning. It's a racy move, albeit with pure motives. When Boaz discovers her asleep at his feet, he symbolically covers her and becomes a picture of redemption. After cultural protocol is followed, Boaz and Ruth eventually marry and bear children. Naomi's inheritance has been restored to her, and Ruth becomes the great-grandmother of King David and an ancestor of the Messiah.

Ruth is a small book with huge themes, a rich picture full of deep truths. It shows us God's heart to restore bitter souls and redeem broken lives. No calamity is beyond His ability to reverse with His goodness. In Naomi, we see someone who had given up find a rewarding place in the eternal plan. In Ruth, we see a foreigner who would be scorned in normal circumstances become an integral part of the people of God simply by showing admirable loyalty and love in an every-man-for-himself era. In Boaz, we see a man with no heirs being given a new bride, a new family, and a fresh start in life. And in God, who quietly authors the story, we see a tender, romantic heart, a provider in hard times, and a Redeemer who has His eye not only on the chosen nation, but also on Gentiles who display His nature and accept His ways. It's a small fulfillment of the covenant He made with Abraham to bless those who bless the Jews. And it's a powerful foreshadowing of how God will draw many into His Kingdom at a harvest festival many centuries later by pouring out His Spirit on Jews and Gentiles alike.

This book is a case study in the scriptural truth that God lifts up the humble and draws near to the brokenhearted. Even in our deepest disappointments, He finds ways to make our lives meaningful and bring us into a place of fulfillment. This process can take a frustratingly long time, but when we demonstrate faith and patience, He makes sure it ends well. And it's always worth the wait.

## QUESTION FOR REFLECTION

In what ways is the story of Ruth and Boaz a picture of our relationship with Jesus?

 DAY 17

# 1 SAMUEL

The book of 1 Samuel describes the journey of a developing monarchy. It isn't an easy journey; the demand for a king is stressful to the ruling priest and bothersome to God. The first king disobeys God and squanders his calling, and the second king must endure a long and painful exile before his reign begins. These three characters—Samuel, the priest and prophet; Saul, the troubled, volatile king; and David, the future king with God's heart—become the focal points of the book. But around the stories of these main characters, numerous subplots, crisis events, and personal conflicts erupt. Israel transitions from an era of turbulent disunity to an era of stable monarchy, though being God's chosen nation doesn't make it immune to corrupt influences, power plays, and intense rivalries. God's people want to be like other nations and have a king. They find that they are like other nations in other, less desirable ways as well.

Though Samuel, Saul, and David dominate the landscape of 1 Samuel, the era of transition is sparked by an unlikely character: a barren woman whose husband's other wife keeps taunting her for being childless. Hannah pleads with God for a son, pledging that she will give him to God to serve as a priest. God answers and Hannah faithfully fulfills her vow. The son is Samuel, who grows up to replace the current priest and his corrupt sons. Although

Samuel warns the people about the danger of monarchy, he presides over the transition from no king to Saul, and then from Saul to David, though he doesn't live long enough to see David become king.

Samuel anoints David after God rejects Saul for rashly disobeying Him on at least two occasions. But there's a long gap between the anointing of David and Saul's death, and David spends much of it on the run. Samuel dies during David's exile, having mourned Saul's regrettable kingship. As Saul rises to power and then falls from grace, growing increasingly unstable—jealousy, rage, and manic-depressive tendencies plague him in his later years—Samuel fades from the story and David becomes the main character. First Samuel describes the rise to power of Israel's archetypal king.

The stories of David's life are well known: He defeats a giant Philistine named Goliath with a slingshot, even though the warrior's taunts had paralyzed Israel's army. He plays music for Saul to soothe the king's volatile spirit. He develops a deep friendship with Saul's son Jonathan. He marries two of Saul's daughters as rewards for his exploits. He flees from Saul's jealous wrath, gathering a group of loyal warriors who travel around the countryside with him. He gets food and supplies from a community of priests, all of whom are later slaughtered for unwittingly aiding Saul's enemy. David feigns insanity in order to live in a Philistine town for a time. He meets a woman named Abigail who persuades him not to take vengeance on her inhospitable husband, who dies just days after encountering David—and David ends up marrying her. He raids villages of Israel's enemies. And he prepares himself to go to war against Saul's armies, even though he has twice refused to kill the king in spite of golden opportunities to do so. The Philistines refuse to fight alongside him, but one wonders what would have happened if they had. Would David have taken up weapons against his own people and his own king? The account in 1 Samuel leaves us hanging.

What is clear throughout these stories of David's years of preparation is that the unlikely shepherd-who-would-be-king has centered his life on God. He is passionate, purposeful, and principled. He will not harm God's anointed, even though God's anointed has vowed to kill him. He cannot bear to hear taunts against the armies of the living God, so he accepts the giant's challenge and risks his life in hand-to-hand combat. He feels responsible for a raid against the camp and families of his men, so he fervently pursues the raiders and recovers everything that was lost. He constantly wears his heart on his sleeve. And, for the most part, his heart relentlessly hungers for God.

The overall effect of this book is to convince us that David is the kind of man God supports. A country in spiritual chaos demands a king and is given one, and the next forty years convince the people that simply having a king isn't enough. The king also has to be good. David, who loves God and follows Him wholeheartedly, rises to the top, while Saul, with a selfish agenda and an independent spirit, has the kingdom ripped from his grasp. The trajectory of these two lives makes a dramatic point: God is searching for devoted followers who are willing to lay themselves on the line for Him. When He finds them, He does whatever it takes to prepare them for greatness and establish them firmly within His plans.

## Questions for Reflection

Why do you think there's such a long gap between David's anointing as king and the time when Saul dies and David actually becomes king? What do you think God accomplished during these years?

## DAY 18

# 2 SAMUEL

David's preparation has lasted a long time. That's always the way it is with God's choicest servants. Abraham waited long years for a child; Joseph endured betrayal, slavery, and prison for years before God fulfilled the dreams He had given him; and Moses spent forty years in exile before being called back to Egypt as Israel's deliverer. Now that David has been proven in the wilderness for years, his time to reign has come.

But it doesn't come immediately. The nation is divided over whether David or Saul's son Ishbosheth should reign. The northern tribes of Israel side with Ishbosheth, while David is anointed king of Judah. A long civil war between the house of David and the house of Saul ensues and eventually ends, but not without some rather messy incidents of betrayal and murder. David is then anointed as king of Israel, too, and the nation is again united.

Second Samuel gives us glimpses of David the worshiper, the man after God's own heart, primarily through his desire to bring the Ark of the Covenant into Jerusalem and also through his desire to build a temple in Jerusalem for God. The journey of the Ark to Jerusalem, the new capital established by David, is a troubled one, as one of its transporters is struck dead simply for touching the holy vessel. When the Ark is eventually brought into the city, David is rebuked by his wife for dancing in a very undignified way with the common people.

His passion to build a temple isn't a smooth process either, as God defers the privilege to the next generation. David can only write about the future project in several psalms, and according to a later chronicler, draw up detailed architectural plans for his unfulfilled dream. Yet David's request to begin the Temple project gives God the occasion to establish David's royal family line forever. It's a promise that will send scholars into a theological crisis during the nation's later captivity and foreign occupations, when no heir of David was anywhere close to sitting on a throne; but the New Testament writers point to the fulfillment of God's promise through a certain descendant of David's born on a holy night in David's hometown of Bethlehem. David's line *is* established eternally—eventually.

Much of 2 Samuel is devoted to the arc of David's military success and its subsequent decline. He wins great victories over the Philistines, Ammonites, Edomites, Moabites, Arameans, and the dreaded Amalekites. But his reign spirals downward into attempted coups from within his own family and plenty of palace intrigue and treachery. The plotline of David's career hinges on one event—his sin with a woman named Bathsheba and his attempted cover-up—after which his house is in almost constant turmoil. The prophet Nathan accuses the king of "stealing a sheep"—taking to his bed the wife of a loyal soldier—and then arranging the soldier's death on the battlefield to cover up the true timing and source of the widow's pregnancy. The child from that pregnancy dies, but the couple's next child becomes the future king, providing a redemptive outcome to a sordid story.

One of the more endearing traits of the Bible's history books is their refusal to idealize their heroes. David is a hero, but a flawed one. He's a man after God's own heart and a passionate worshiper, but one who makes some bad decisions and provokes frequent controversy. Far more than just Bathsheba's husband, many people die on David's account: a community of priests in Nob (from his fugitive years in 1 Samuel), leaders of rival factions battling over his kingship, and even 70,000 citizens after he takes an ill-advised census and God judges him for it. Yet David becomes Israel's archetypal king, a picture of the future Messiah (who, contrary to David, doesn't fall into sin), and a model of how to have an authentic relationship with God that is brutally honest in its desires, passions, regrets, and repentance. If we learn anything from David's life, it's that God loves those who pursue Him wholeheartedly, perhaps even recklessly, without any pretense of perfection. "Son of David" becomes an epithet for the Messiah, because for all his faults, David loves God more than anyone or anything. That's a picture of the heart of the faultless Messiah, as well as a picture of the hearts of those who choose to follow Him. No matter how messy our lives become, living with that kind of passion will always bring pleasure to God.

## QUESTIONS FOR REFLECTION

What does it mean to be someone after God's own heart? What did that look like in David's life? What does it look like in yours?

 DAY 19

# 1 KINGS

The Lord loved Solomon. That's what 2 Samuel 12:24 tells us after Solomon is born to David and Bathsheba, the royal couple whose marriage began in scandal. David loved his son, too, and had picked him as his successor. But as 1 Kings opens, David dies and another one of his sons prepares to assume the throne. The resulting conflict reveals a surprising ruthlessness in Solomon as he purges his rivals from the kingdom. Pretty quickly, the kingdom is firmly in Solomon's hands.

But Solomon doesn't have the same heart as his father did. There are plenty of admirable things about him—his wisdom, for example. In a dream at the altar of Gibeon, where Solomon has offered a thousand sacrifices because of his love for the Lord,

God gives him an extravagant offer to ask for anything he wants. Because Solomon chooses wisdom and understanding over wealth and power, God gives him "all of the above." The king goes on to make wise judgments, as when two prostitutes go to court over which is the mother of a child. He writes proverbs and songs numbering in the thousands. His fame extends far into other nations, as exemplified by a queen from Sheba who comes to visit and marvel at the glory of his kingdom. But he has his faults, too, and unlike his father's, they involve long-term neglect of God's clear instructions. He marries numerous foreign wives in order to form national alliances, a practice firmly forbidden in the Law. He acquires horses and other military resources from Egypt, also forbidden by the Law. He burdens his people with forced labor (though 1 Kings 9:22 emphasizes that it wasn't equal to slavery). Near the end of his life, he begins building and worshiping at pagan altars constructed at his wives' requests and associated with vile practices. He becomes deeply disappointed with the fleeting and superficial nature of life—a wise man who violates his own proverbs and suffers the consequences of his own warnings. He's an unsettling example of someone who starts well and ends up corrupted and disillusioned.

Yet Solomon's reign is considered the golden age of Israel's nationhood. The king whose name means "peace" (from *shalom*) extends his borders and has peace on every side. In this era of stability, he is able to build the Temple God had promised he would build and construct a massive palace. It's just a brief season of glory in Israel's history; the nation divides after Solomon's death and descends into long generations of idolatry and warfare. But for a moment, Israel is a shining example of how God can bless a kingdom.

About seventy years after Solomon's death, when the northern kingdom of Israel is steeped in extreme idolatry under King Ahab and his queen—a thoroughly pagan priestess named Jezebel—an enigmatic prophet named Elijah steps in and declares a drought, a consequence for disobedience given in Deuteronomy 28. After three years without rain, Elijah stages a spiritual showdown on Mount Carmel between himself and the priests of Baal. Baal is impotent to strike the priests' altar with fire, but the true God engulfs Elijah's drenched altar in flames. The people see firsthand which God has real power, and they turn, at least superficially, back to Him. But the king and queen don't, even after a torrential downpour ends the drought, and so Elijah flees for his life. God has called His people back to Him and many have responded, but the nation remains largely unchanged.

First Kings beautifully captures the highs and lows of being fallen creatures in relationship with a powerful God. At our best, we seek wisdom like Solomon, desire the glory of a temple filled with God's presence, dedicate our greatest undertakings to His purposes, and experience the power of being wholeheartedly devoted to Him. At other times, our greatest encounters with God are followed by the fickleness of Solomon, the depression of Elijah, or even the blatant idolatry of a blessed nation. We go to great and noble depths with our God, even while remaining capable of neglecting or even forsaking Him. We live in this tension, knowing that He is always calling us higher, and as He made clear at Solomon's dedication ceremony, wanting His presence to dwell among us and within us. In 1 Kings, we see human beings reaching out to God, God reaching out to human beings, and the fallen nature of humanity severing the relationship again and again. But we also know of a greater Temple and a truer altar—and of a God who, even after all these centuries of history, is still zealous to live in our midst.

## QUESTIONS FOR REFLECTION

How do you think someone as wise as Solomon ended up disillusioned and depressed? Why did his wisdom not lead to fulfillment and satisfaction?

DAY 20

# 2 KINGS

First Kings is the story of a nation divided and in decline. Second Kings continues the story all the way to its tragic end—the fall of the nation. That fall occurs in two cataclysmic stages, with Assyria conquering the northern kingdom of Israel and Babylon sacking the southern kingdom of Judah more than a century later. For a nation that was given extravagant promises backed by the power of God Himself, this is not only a national disaster but also a theological crisis. God has let His people be forsaken. Why?

The answer to that question comes through the mouths of many prophets, whose writings we will explore later. But not all the major prophets wrote their prophecies, Elijah and Elisha being the primary examples. Just as 1 Kings ends with the ministry of Elijah, 2 Kings begins with the transition from the older prophet to his protégé, Elisha, who accompanies his mentor across the Jordan, is separated from him by a chariot of fire, and watches Elijah taken up to heaven in a whirlwind. Elisha, having asked for a double portion of Elijah's spirit—his power, influence, and anointing—finds that the request has been granted.

The whole transition is rather symbolic; the two prophets take a path out of the Promised Land that almost exactly resembles the path Joshua and the Israelites had taken into it centuries earlier. And then Elisha recrosses the Jordan into the land at virtually the same spot as the first entrance. It's as if God is saying, "Let's try this again." In fact, that's what our relationship with God is often like. We fail, but He brings us into new opportunities to succeed.

In many ways, this is the theme of the historical books of Hebrew Scripture. In 2 Kings, we see God's people flailing under a broken covenant, with a few sporadic and noble attempts to restore themselves to the blessings of that covenant. Good kings, such as Joash, Hezekiah, and Josiah, are noteworthy, not only because they try to reform the nation and rededicate it to God, ridding the land of false worship (albeit in varying degrees), but also because they are exceptional leaders—countercultural catalysts for change who are often portrayed as swimming against social currents while trying to flow with the Spirit of God. They are brief bright spots in an otherwise bleak history as God's patience is stretched and tested by the many other kings who do not live up to the covenant (and at times, even scoff at it).

This is the culture in which Elisha comes of age. Having inherited a double portion of Elijah's spirit, he performs twice as many recorded miracles as Elijah, many of which foreshadow miracles the Messiah will do centuries later. He reverses a curse on Jericho by purifying its water, resurrects a woman's only son, heals a Gentile of leprosy, and pulls back the curtain on the unseen world so his servant can see the armies of God. Elisha is somewhat of a warning signal for the northern kingdom, yet its kings continue to ignore God and pursue their own idols and agendas. The result is a dramatic picture of a broken covenant. Unlike the chroniclers of other nations who whitewash their kings' exploits and accomplishments, Israel's historians are bluntly honest about their kings' ungodliness and its consequences. And unlike other chroniclers, Israel's historians assess their kings not on how many battles they win or how much influence they have, but on whether they worship the true God with a pure heart. None of the kings of the northern kingdom submit themselves to God, so He allows Assyria to conquer Israel and disperse its people. They will never be a separate nation, "holy to the Lord," again.

The southern kingdom of Judah takes a longer path toward captivity—at least a few of its kings make noble efforts at reform and faithfulness—but its people are eventually exiled as Jerusalem and its sacred Temple, the dwelling place of God, lie in ruins. Many of the people will return, as the prophets have foretold, and rebuild Jerusalem as a remnant of the chosen nation. In fact, 2 Kings ends with a reference to a surviving descendant of David's, Jehoiachin, a muted hint that God's promise of establishing David's throne may still be alive. But it's a slim remnant. At the end of 2 Kings, the chosen nation isn't looking very chosen.

That's always how it appears when our dreams and destinies come crashing down around us. God's promise may seem faint or even completely forfeited. But the restoration He promised for this broken world in Genesis, promised for the rebellious nation of Israel in the Law, and prophesied for His captive people in the Prophets, is still high on God's agenda. He doesn't begin projects that He won't complete. That's true of the world as a whole, of the collective peoples He has called, and of the individual lives He has redeemed. If He has begun a good work in us or among us, He will perfect it—in time, in spite of crises, and even when our theology or our faith can't imagine how. He may let us fall, but never out of His reach. And He never abandons His plan.

## Questions for Reflection

How do you think you would have responded to prophets such as Elijah and Elisha? What do they tell us about the way God speaks? What do their interactions with Israel tell us about the way people respond?

DAY 21

# 1 CHRONICLES

The books of 1 and 2 Chronicles don't drive the plot of Scripture forward. Instead, they supply nuance and meaning to Israel's history by looking at it from a different angle. From the genealogies, cultural commentary, and theological perspective in these books, we can tell that they were written long after the Exile; but they review events leading up to the Exile—primarily from the time of David forward. In fact, the focus on the life of David is the key to understanding both books. The chronicler sees God's covenant with David as the centerpiece of the nation's destiny. From a post-Exile point of view, these books look back in order to look forward.

Because of the focus on David and his line of succession, 1 and 2 Chronicles include many of the same events we've read about in Samuel and Kings: David's military exploits, his desire to bring the Ark of the Covenant into Jerusalem, his setting up of the Tabernacle in the Holy City. The book begins with extended genealogies leading up to David's family and extending beyond it, all the way through the captivity in Babylon and the return to Jerusalem. But this is only Judah's history; by the time the Chronicles are written, the northern Israelites have been dispersed and have intermarried and assimilated with Assyrian culture. First Chronicles thus becomes a rallying point for Judah to regain the significance of God's covenant and be established as a faithful remnant. This is the story of a chastened and fragmented people coming back together in order to be God's set-apart people again—this time with renewed vision and commitment.

First Chronicles devotes a lot of attention to how the priests and musicians were assigned to lead the nation's worship and how God blessed the kingdom for this devotional focus. It highlights

God's promise to establish David's royal line forever and for his successor to build the Temple. It gives much greater detail to the transition between David and Solomon, with emphasis on how David challenged the nation spiritually and charged his son with carrying the divine mission forward, even providing detailed architectural and liturgical plans for the worship center.

In its redemptive focus, 1 Chronicles simply describes David's military successes, without mentioning his sin with Bathsheba, the cover-up, and the messy aftermath. There is no need to explain the sins of the fathers at this point; the nation has already been chastised enough for them. In fact, the chronicler reflects a subtle theological adjustment: He shifts the blame for bad things onto Satan rather than attributing them to God the Judge. For example, 2 Samuel 24:1 says the Lord incited David to take a census; 1 Chronicles 21:1 says that Satan incited him to do it. This development forces us to view spiritual history in more layered, complex terms, opening our eyes to another dimension of conflict between God and His enemies. Through all the years of all the kings' reigns leading up to the Exile, Israel didn't just fail to keep God's covenant; they lost a spiritual battle. In other words, they had some unholy help.

So, 1 and 2 Chronicles don't simply recap Israel's history—they spiritualize it. On the one hand, David the godly king pursues God wholeheartedly and aims to establish the nation in its God-given role as priest to other nations—the divine link between God and a broken world. But forces of idolatry, fueled not only by the fickle hearts of human beings, but also by malevolent spirits in an unseen realm, rage violently against God's people. David's Tabernacle and Solomon's Temple are *needed*. The true worship of God is at stake. We are left with admiration for the godly king and the awareness of a God who wants to be present with His people. This presence, according to the chronicler's theology, seems to be the overarching purpose behind the covenant.

These are good themes to embrace. Creation was never about God finding more servants. It's about relationship. It's the story of a God who wants to share Himself with people who can relate to Him on multiple levels: intellectually, emotionally, spiritually, and even at times physically through our very tangible modes of worship and His very tangible responses. All of biblical history up to this point and beyond shows us what a battle this is. In a sense, the trajectory of all of Scripture is a response to the issues raised in Eden: Is God really good? Has He really said what you think He said? Are you really like Him? The connection that was lost in the Garden is being reestablished, and God's covenant with David and each phase of His dwelling place are vital keys. The more we enter into God's covenant and seek His presence, the more we will experience His Kingdom in our lives.

## QUESTIONS FOR REFLECTION

Why do you think David was so passionate about his desire to build a temple? What did he want for it to accomplish?

 DAY 22

# 2 CHRONICLES

As much as the Chronicles idealize David as a positive example to follow, the books also give us plenty of examples not to follow. They commend the things that keep people and countries in right relationship with God while condemning the things that separate us from Him and repel the divine presence. It all boils down to a single dynamic: who or what we choose to worship.

That's why the Temple of God and the high places of idolatry are so prevalent in Scripture. Worshiping the true God—and by implication, doing what He says as an act of our worship—brings life and blessing, just as the Torah already told us. Worshiping idols and disobeying God brings death and destruction. We often see both dynamics in the same person. Some kings begin well and end poorly. Some begin poorly but end well. And some reap the consequences of lifelong rebellion. These are spiritual hero-and-villain stories, all tied to the welfare of the nation of Judah. And as we have seen, they end in catastrophe.

Well, almost. The catastrophe isn't total, and it isn't quite the end. The saga almost ends with 2 Chronicles 36:15-16: "The LORD, the God of their ancestors, repeatedly sent his prophets to warn them, for he had compassion on his people and his Temple. But the people mocked these messengers of God and despised their words. They scoffed at the prophets until the LORD's anger could no longer be restrained and nothing could be done." But there is a brief epilogue (2 Chronicles 36:17-23) that reminds us that even though Jerusalem was reduced to rubble, the captivity fulfilled a designated seventy-year exile foretold by Jeremiah the prophet, and that Cyrus of Persia issued a proclamation to allow the exiles of Judah to return to the land. So in spite of the crisis, there's hope.

Even before the epic ending, we see other glimpses of hope along the way. King Asa is a reformer who tries to purge the nation of idolatry and depends on God in battles, and God defends him. When Asa begins to rely on his own strength, a prophet reminds him of the key principle for success: "The eyes of the LORD search the whole earth in order to strengthen those whose hearts are fully committed to him" (2 Chronicles 16:9). God responds with ample aid for those who are wholeheartedly devoted to Him. We see this truth at work again with the very next king, Jehoshaphat, who is surrounded by a vast coalition of enemy warriors and cries out to God for help. A prophet is inspired to declare that the battle is the Lord's, not the people's, and that all they have to do in the battle is stand still and see God's salvation. A choir of worshipers leads the warriors into battle, and God prompts their enemies to turn against each other. His people acknowledge their weakness and simply praise Him, and He fights for them. Yet for some reason, many generations of Israelites—and God's people throughout history—forget this truth and rely on their own resources and reasoning.

That's certainly true of the generations of kings after Jehoshaphat, but finally Hezekiah reinstitutes Temple worship and celebrates Passover, which apparently has been long neglected. This commitment to Judah's worship life attracts God's favor, and when a blasphemous, seemingly invincible king of Assyria surrounds Jerusalem, making arrogant threats, Hezekiah cries out and God intervenes. At the last minute, when all seems lost, God turns the Assyrians away, making sure they never come back.

Years later, as King Josiah turns the nation back to true worship, the book of Moses' Law is found by a priest while repairs are being made on the Temple. It's a landmark discovery that brings both grief (because the Law has been long neglected) and joy (because it has been found). Yet even this isn't enough to save the country from God's judgment; subsequent generations again turn away from God, in spite of the Law's clear instructions.

In all these biographies—the good and the bad—we get glimpses of Israel's history at a personal level. Granted, it's a court history, the stories of royals and generals rather than the stories of everyday people; but it's still a series of personal biographies that reveal very human struggles. The welfare of the nation is at stake, and that welfare is shaped by the thoughts and behaviors of individuals. What makes the difference in all these people's lives is how they relate to God. That defines everything—success or failure, peace or war, joy or grief. Those who zealously cultivate their love for God are blessed.

## Questions for Reflection

Why is worship such a critical issue in Scripture? Why did Israel keep turning to idols? How did God keep prompting them to turn back to Him? What does worship of God accomplish in our lives?

 DAY 23

# EZRA

Despite all the devastation inflicted on Judah by the Babylonians, God has the conquering empire on a leash. In other words, Judah's captivity is for a limited time, subject to God's sovereign judgment. In accordance with Jeremiah's prophecies, the Exile lasts seventy years and ends when Cyrus, the king of Persia, who has overthrown Babylon, issues a decree that any willing Jews can return to their native land. Some 40,000 choose to do so, though many others have settled throughout the known world and choose to remain where they are. Those who return face a daunting task: rebuilding Jerusalem and the Temple.

So the story of restoration begins. God's people, harshly disciplined for centuries of betraying their covenant with Him, not only have decades of rebuilding in front of them, but also have to deal with rebuilding a relationship with their Creator. If unfaithfulness led to such displeasure from God that He let the pagan Babylonians carry His people into exile, then surely a first step back would be a recommitment to faithfulness. If idolatry grieved God's heart, then a necessary gesture would be to reestablish true worship. And these are the steps the returnees take.

But it isn't a quick process. Zerubbabel and Jeshua lead a first wave of exiles home and almost immediately begin sacrificing on the site of the old altar. They also lay a foundation for rebuilding the Temple. The work is interrupted by opponents in the land, who send formal complaints to the king, charging the Jews with being tax-delinquent troublemakers and rebels. Eventually, Darius, a successor to Cyrus, is urged to look up the original decree, and the rebuilding continues. The Temple is dedicated and the people rejoice.

Some seventy or eighty years later, a scribe named Ezra is sent with a second wave of returnees from Babylon to preside over the reimplementation of God's law. He finds an active worship life among his people, but he is also alarmed at the number who have married foreign women—non-Jews from the remaining Canaanite population and from surrounding nations. The issue isn't the ethnicity of their wives (foreigners who convert to Judaism have always been grafted into God's people); the issue is worship, specifically the temptation for a man to worship his wife's gods. Thus, intermarriage becomes a major crisis, as the worship of foreign gods was one of the key offenses that caused God to judge His people in the first place. People just returning from exile shouldn't commit the same sins that led to their exile. The leaders convene and agree that this practice must be stopped. They decide that the foreign wives and their children must be sent away.

These are drastic measures, but the people recently chastised by God find themselves very sensitive to issues of right and wrong. They have found out the hard way that offending God causes a lot of grief. Meanwhile, God has made it clear that He is more interested in their love than in their legalities. Yes, He wants His law to be obeyed, but obedience is only meaningful when it's the response of a loving heart. He wants the relationship restored to new depths.

We see glimpses of tender hearts in this story, particularly when the foundation of the Temple is laid. Some of the older people, who remember Jerusalem before its destruction, begin to weep, and others begin to shout with joy. They are, as a psalm describes them, "like those who dream" (Psalm 126:1, NKJV). Their seventy-year sorrow has finally been addressed by the God who restores.

This scene strikes a chord in us because we all long to have our dreams fulfilled. The return of Judah from exile points us in that direction; it's a picture of the great restoration that is coming when Jesus fully establishes His Kingdom. We've seen many scriptural glimpses of unbridled joy—Abraham and Sarah's child of laughter, the celebration on the safe side of the Red Sea, the entrance into the Promised Land, Ruth's marriage and Naomi's vindication, Hannah's answered prayer for a child, the dedication of the Temple, and more. Our tears well up when we see someone celebrate a dream come true because it taps into our deepest longings. We want God to be our dream fulfiller too. The message of Scripture is that He is. The coming of His Kingdom into our lives is very good news. In one way or another, sooner or later, He fills our hearts with joy.

## QUESTIONS FOR REFLECTION

Have you experienced God as a restorer? If so, how? What have you learned about Him in the restoration process? How has it changed you and deepened your relationship with Him?

 DAY 24

# NEHEMIAH

While Ezra works to reestablish Jerusalem as a worship center for the one true God and the people of Judah as God's set-apart nation, Nehemiah is serving in the Persian capital as a high-ranking official in the king's court. When some travelers from Judah bring him a discouraging report about the conditions there—the returnees are struggling and the city is in disrepair—Nehemiah is greatly disturbed. In response, he prays and fasts with urgency and deep conviction. His prayer is a model of intercession, as well as an example of how God moves through the passions of His people. Apparently, Nehemiah's demeanor is affected; the king asks him why he is so sad. Nehemiah's explanation prompts the king to authorize and fund a mission to repair Jerusalem's walls, with Nehemiah leading the venture. Edict in hand, Nehemiah organizes a contingent to go to Jerusalem and rebuild.

What follows is a classic case study in how God works through His people—and how enemies and obstacles rise up in opposition. A couple of instigators and their followers try a number of tactics, including direct confrontation, intimidation, slander, conspiracy, distraction, and manipulation, to hinder the rebuilding process. It's a dramatic picture of a fallen world's hostility toward the building of God's Kingdom. In every kind of attack, Nehemiah and his coworkers demonstrate unwavering persistence and single-minded commitment to the task. They are vigilant in their response, at times simply refusing to believe lies or cave in to fear, at other times standing guard day and night to protect the laborers against violent attack. They resolutely refuse to allow the harassment to knock them off course, working together toward the ultimate goal.

Not all of the threats toward this rebuilding community are external. Many of the Jews who have returned to the land are suffering economic hardship, and their wealthier kinsmen are helping them out with loans—at very profitable interest rates. The result is virtual servitude for the borrowers, a condition that violates God's purposes for His people. Citing his own personal sacrifices on behalf of the people, Nehemiah urges the lenders to repent, which includes the return of all mortgaged property to the borrowers.

After the wall is rebuilt, Nehemiah and Ezra reinstitute God's law and lead the people in recommitting to God's covenant. When the Law is read for everyone to hear, the people weep; they realize how grievously they and their forebears have neglected the words of God. Yet Nehemiah and the priests speak only words of encouragement. After all, it's the joy of the Lord that gives His people strength.

Later, at the dedication of the rebuilt wall, the joy of the people is heard far away. They have ceased looking back at the sins of the nation and are looking ahead toward the bright days of the newly established city of God—a place they have committed to the true worship of God and the ethical treatment of neighbors. Like Ezra, Nehemiah deals harshly with those who have married foreign, nonbelieving wives, even with physical force. In fact, all Ammonites and Moabites, nations that refused to aid Israel on its way to the Promised Land, are shunned from the community as the law of Moses dictates—perhaps the story of Ruth the Moabite has been long forgotten. And Sabbath breakers are promised a severe punishment if they continue in their work on the holy day. The purity of this community is paramount to its leaders, and the preservation of that purity begins to develop a hard edge.

Nehemiah is often held up as a model of godly leadership (though most leadership courses leave out the part about his cursing, beating, and pulling out the hair of those who had married pagan wives). And it's true that his strong, unwavering commitment to the task was vital to its completion. He was truly on assignment from God, who had put His will into Nehemiah's heart. But this era of rebuilding raises questions about what it means to be a community where God's presence dwells. Where is the line between law and grace? How do we implement God's requirements in our lives without becoming motivated by obligation rather than by love? How do flawed people reflect a holy God? Judaism will wrestle with these questions for the centuries after Ezra and Nehemiah, and we continue to wrestle with them today. God is perfect, we are not, and the gap between us begs to be bridged.

## QUESTIONS FOR REFLECTION

What does Nehemiah teach us about persistence in accomplishing God's will? What does he teach us about handling conflict and eliminating distractions? Why are these things necessary in our walk with God?

 DAY 25

# ESTHER

Unlike Ezra and Nehemiah, the book of Esther doesn't focus on Jewish distinctives and laws, such as dietary restrictions, sacred feasts, or intermarriage with foreigners. It doesn't even mention God. Its purpose is directed not at restoring God's people in Judah and Jerusalem but at encouraging those who have remained scattered across the empire. These Jews, far outnumbering those who went back to Judah, have adapted to a wide variety of languages and cultures, some assimilating and others remaining defiantly unassimilated. They are a part of the societal mix of the Persian Empire.

As in Europe in the 1930s, there were some in Persia who didn't want Jews to be part of the societal mix—most notably the king's right-hand man, Haman, a narcissistic descendant of an Amalekite king. Israel's King Saul had disobeyed God's command to destroy the Amalekites centuries earlier, and now the bitter ethnic rivalry between the two groups plays out between Haman and Mordecai, a Jew who seems to have some position of influence in or around the palace. Mordecai refuses to bow to Haman, and Haman is so outraged that he plots to "destroy, kill, and annihilate" the entire Jewish race. What he doesn't know is that Queen Esther, a young

Jewish woman originally named Hadassah, who had been chosen by the king several years earlier to replace his previous wife, is actually a relative of Mordecai's. Esther's nervous acceptance of her key role in saving her people becomes a hinge moment, the kind on which the doors of history frequently swing. She is there "for just such a time as this" (Esther 4:14), which happens to be a critical moment that threatens God's people—and God's entire salvation plan—with extinction.

The story that follows is filled with ironic twists and sudden reversals of fortune, as Esther gradually unveils the plot (and her ethnic identity) to the king. In his pride, Haman envisions himself as the most powerful man in the kingdom, and in his fall (which, according to Scripture, always seems to follow pride), he and his sons are executed on the very same gallows that were meant to be a curse for Israel. The tables are completely turned, an age-old divine decree against the Amalekites is fulfilled, and Mordecai the Jew is elevated into Haman's vacant position of power. This decisive vindication is wildly celebrated by the Jews in a festival known as Purim—still the most joyful holiday on the Jewish calendar.

Though the events of Esther seem to be clearly orchestrated by God, who will not see His plans thwarted or His people wiped out, the fact that the book never mentions Him or His intervention makes a powerful statement. We too must read between the lines of our lives and decide whether our circumstances are merely random or overseen by a sovereign God. No commentator spells that out for us as we're going through our trials; we are left to simply trust and act on what we know to be true. In the face of overwhelming crises, we must choose whether to expect the worst or believe that God is faithful to His promises. Like Esther, we must stand between fear and faith in crisis moments and realize the opportunity and position God has placed us in, knowing that our responses are hinges on which God's story swings. Most of all, we can count on the fact that no situation is hopeless, no matter how it appears, and that God is capable of sudden reversals that turn apparent defeats into victories, mourning into dancing, and death into resurrection. These are the victories that fill not only His Word, but even our lives.

## QUESTIONS FOR REFLECTION

In what ways do we have to "read between the lines" of our lives to see God? Do you tend to see circumstances as arranged by God or as the results of human decisions—or both? Why?

 DAY 26

# JOB

Some people think the message of Job is that God doesn't put a hedge of protection around His people. But a careful reading of the story reveals that He did have a hedge of protection around Job and only removed it temporarily. Likewise, some people believe the message of Job is that human suffering is a mystery with no rhyme or reason or acceptable theological explanation, though the first chapter clearly explains why Job suffers. The explanation is hidden to him, even at the end of the story, but the reader sees it plainly. No, the messages in Job are far more nuanced—and deeper—than many casual readers realize.

In the broadest terms, we can say that human suffering has a purpose, but we often don't know what it is. In Job's case, he becomes the subject of the adversary's bet against God, and God willingly allows one of His choicest servants to play that painful role—not because God is unjust or sadistic, but because there are higher stakes than Job's immediate welfare. The real theological issue in this book is whether God can be worshiped for His goodness even when His goodness seems to go into hiding. The adversary—literally, the *satan*—believes Job's faithfulness is superficially dependent on the blessings he has received. God says it's deeper than that. If this faithful follower can continue to worship and follow even when every blessing in his life seems to have been removed, God is glorified and the adversary's accusations are proven wrong. And that's what's at stake: a statement of God's glory. Job pays a temporary price for it and will be amply rewarded in the end. In the meantime, he suffers excruciating pain and rejection and has his faith stretched nearly beyond its limits.

Job's friends become the theological focal point of this book. They are often criticized for their bad belief system, but few people realize how often they accurately quote biblical principles in their arguments with Job. Perhaps that's why they are so easily and often quoted; readers see truth in their statements and lift them out of context, not realizing that these babblers are rebuked in the end for everything they say. But what they say fits well with the blessings and curses of Deuteronomy 28, as well as with the proverbs written by Solomon, and the dynamics we see throughout the historical books that God blesses those who are obedient to Him and withdraws His blessing from those who aren't. These are rock-solid biblical truths, but after Job's friends quote them, they are chastised by God. Why? Because truth applied at the wrong time in the wrong situation isn't truth. And Job's friends are shallow enough not to ask God what He is doing in the situation. Like many believers today, they have the Word and they apply it across the board. There's no need to hear God's voice if you have a cookie-cutter spirituality, a set of biblical principles to live by. But in the book of Job, that approach is thoroughly rejected.

The truth is that our relationships with God are relationships *with Him*, not with a set of principles—even biblical ones. We have to be able to hear His voice and discern His purposes, even when we think we already have a handle on His precepts. Truth that applies in one situation may not apply in another. It depends on the season of a person's life and what God is doing in it.

At the end of the story, Job is both rebuked and vindicated. He has an encounter with God that brings him to his knees, yet his friends (all but the enigmatic Elihu, who may have expressed God's truth better than the others) are chastened for their ignorant preaching. And Job's blessings are restored—doubly so. He receives back exactly two times what he lost, except for the number of children, which remains the same. (This is perhaps because his deceased children still live in the afterlife; so an equal number of children doubles the total.) Job's life after his trials is a picture of Paul's later statement that the cost of our temporary trials will never outweigh the benefits of eternal glory (2 Corinthians 4:17). Whatever hardships we go through now will fade in comparison to the blessings we receive at the end—even if we don't understand why we are going through such trouble. There's a divine drama behind the events of our lives, and God will ultimately be glorified. Looking back one day, we will be glad for the part we played in that drama—and doubly blessed for it.

## Questions for Reflection

Under what circumstances are you most likely to question God's goodness? Why must our worship of Him never be contingent on circumstances? Why is it wrong to apply uniform scriptural explanations to the trials we or others face?

DAY 27

# PSALMS 1–41

Thus far in Scripture, we've seen God create the world and a race of people who are made in His image in order to develop a relationship with them. We've seen that race of people break the relationship, become rebels and wanderers, and then be wooed back into relationship with God through a chosen individual, then a family, and then a nation. We've seen God crave being present among His people and His people crave His presence—especially when they're in need. And we've seen an overarching mission to subdue the earth and all that is wrong in it—a Kingdom purpose that will only be accomplished when a righteous King comes. In short, we have seen a shattered creation undergoing a long process of restoration.

This is a traumatic process, and the trauma is nowhere more evident than in the Psalms. These poems and songs—the worship book of ancient Israel—portray the full range of human emotion, which seems to bleed onto the page from the hearts of passionate writers. They express the pain and promise of a broken past and fulfilling future, the angst of appealing to an invisible God for help with very visible crises, the stretching and hammering and molding of faith, the unbridled joy of experiencing a God who fulfills dreams and destinies. Virtually anything we feel in our lives today has been expressed in a Hebrew psalm. It's all poured out in blunt honesty before a God who can handle it.

The Hebrew psalter contains 150 psalms divided into five "books," though the books are not grouped by topic, theme, writer, or any other discernible criteria. The first book comprises Psalms 1–41, many of which can be tied to specific events in Scripture. Many of the psalms are attributed to David, but certainly not all. And they reflect on God's greatest feats (e.g., Creation, the Exodus) as well as humanity's greatest weaknesses (e.g., powerless to defend, needing rescue). Those that begin in crisis almost always end in praise; they are a field manual for how to get from point A to point B in our spiritual and emotional lives, as well as in our circumstances. We cry out, we come to a place of faith and trust, God intervenes, and we praise Him for His goodness. This is very often the trajectory of the psalmist's cry, whether a psalmist of ancient Israel or the one in our own hearts. We relate to these psalms because the voices behind them thoroughly capture human experience. And God has given them to us as Scripture because His presence in them is a thoroughly divine response.

The best-known psalm in this first section is Psalm 23, the shepherd's verse written by King David. But there are other well-known passages in this first book as well: a messianic prophecy claiming influence over all nations (Psalm 2); a creation psalm celebrating the mystery of our existence (Psalm 8); a deliverance psalm hearkening back to Exodus imagery (Psalm 18); a lament of forsakenness that will be quoted by the Messiah from the cross (Psalm 22); a Davidic psalm of seeking after God and being certain of His rescue and His goodness, even in this life (Psalm 27); a Davidic dedication psalm for the Temple, which wouldn't be built until the next generation (Psalm 30); a joyful celebration that God's goodness can be tasted and seen (Psalm 34); and a wisdom psalm about living in the land and seeing one's desires fulfilled because of God's faithfulness (Psalm 37). Interspersed are desperate pleas, patient waiting, bitterness, joy, confession and forgiveness, and much gratitude for overcoming enemies or getting out of trouble.

Millions have found these psalms a source of great comfort—because, after all, where else can you so often find both impossible situations and unwavering hope within a few short verses? These experiences poured out in poetry resonate with us because we go through impossible crises and need assurances of certain hope. We need a God who will intervene with comfort and power and purpose. One of the best ways to stir up faith in God is to read the words of psalmists who experienced Him as profoundly as we desire to.

## QUESTIONS FOR REFLECTION

What do the Psalms tell us about the ways we approach God and the attitudes we're allowed to bring with us? Why do you think God inspired psalms that express such a wide range of human emotion?

 DAY 28

# PSALMS 42–72

Centuries after the Psalms were written, the disciples came to Jesus and asked Him to teach them how to pray. He gave them a sample—we know it as the Lord's Prayer—but He also gave them glimpses of His own prayer life at times. And, not surprisingly, His prayers contained quotes from the Psalms.

Many of the Psalms are horizontal conversations—human beings talking *about* God—but many are vertical conversations—humans speaking *to* God. They therefore serve as a Spirit-inspired reference point for how to pray, a collection of laments and praises and petitions that have functioned as Israel's book of hymns and meditations. They are the prayer language of God's people.

That's why many throughout history have jump-started their conversations with God by finding a psalm that reflects their situation or attitude and praying it. There's something reassuring about praying God's Word back to Him, knowing that it poured from a Spirit-led heart in the past and that God has included it in His revelation. So when we read in Psalm 42 how David thirsts for God as a deer pants for water, or how his own soul is unreasonably discouraged in light of the hope God offers, we can relate and we can echo those words as our own. When we see in Psalm 46 a declaration that God is our refuge and strength, or we hear God's command to be still and know that He is God, we can incorporate both the plea and God's response into our conversation with Him. And when we wonder if we've blown it too badly for God to show us His favor, we can pray David's confession and repentance in Psalm 51, knowing that God's mercy was sufficient to cover a king who was guilty of immorality and murder. When we can't find the words we want to pray, we can turn to the Psalms for help.

The Psalms are also a rebuke to the sanitized prayer lives of those who think they must impress God with their holiness and spiritual-sounding words. The psalmists' words reflect the mess of the human condition and the raw nerves of the soul. They show us that there's no point in hiding from God when we approach Him, as if hiding were a possibility in the first place. We serve a God who has seen it all—literally—and our conversations don't really engage Him until they are completely honest. In fact, our blunt honesty with God—about our flaws and weaknesses, our dreams and desires, and everything else—functions as an invitation for Him to step into our lives. He responds to our transparency because it puts us on the same page with what He already knows. When we are thoroughly authentic, no matter how ugly or stressful our lives, we are ready to grow and change.

This is the model Scripture gives us, though religious minds throughout history have often tried to clean it up. We should be profoundly encouraged that God, who has pursued a relationship with us ever since Eden, has made Himself approachable. If we are raw and real enough to bring our messes to Him, we will experience His welcome. He won't leave us in disarray—He relentlessly draws us closer to Himself, which requires dramatic growth into His likeness. But any starting point is acceptable to Him. He already paid an enormous price to make our approach possible.

Those who wish to commune with God in spirit and truth do well to immerse themselves in the language He prefers. That language is full of the words, images, metaphors, tears, groans, and feelings of the Psalms. This is where God meets us—at our point of need or our moment of celebration and in our hunger for Him. When we seek Him on those terms, He reveals Himself in our circumstances and in the depths of our hearts.

## QUESTIONS FOR REFLECTION

How honest are you with God in your prayers? In what ways can the Psalms help us pray when we don't know what to say to God?

 DAY 29

# PSALMS 73–89

Some Christians think it's unspiritual to be discouraged or disappointed or sad. There's some truth to their point of view; sometimes we have those attitudes because we listen to lies, have distorted perspectives, and don't cultivate the faith and hope God offers us. But sometimes those attitudes come simply because we live in a fallen world. Sometimes dreams are shattered. Sometimes we are overwhelmed with the weight of our circumstances. Sometimes life hurts. And to put on a smile at those times—one that's not a result of the Spirit of hope or peace within us but just to "act spiritual" —is insincere.

The Psalms offer us plenty of examples of laments, a lost art in today's spiritual climate. In Psalm 73, Asaph is able to express his alarm that the wicked seem to prosper and the righteous seem to suffer, to question God about that enigma, and to get an eternal perspective on the issue by getting into God's presence. In Psalm 74, he is able to ask why God seems to have cast off His people forever and appeal to God to be Israel's defender. In Psalm 79, he grieves the destruction of Jerusalem and its seeming abandonment by God, pleading for forgiveness for the nation's sins and asking for vindication against oppressive enemies. Mixed among these laments are psalms of celebration and great joy—Psalm 78 reviews Israel's history with God, for example, and Psalm 84 is one of the most eloquent worship passages in Scripture. A lament in Scripture is never a one-sided picture; among God's people, it's always a temporary sadness. But the sadness is real, the problems are huge, and God sometimes seems too far removed from them. The psalmists pour out their anguish over the human condition, and God grieves with them.

Few people know how to lament well. We either cover our pain with superficial positive thinking or we let our laments descend into grumbling and complaining and despair. Neither is an appropriate response to our brokenness. Somehow we need to acknowledge that life in a fallen world hurts, that things don't always work out, and that human suffering is a brutal part of our existence. But we need to do it without blaming God, or on the other hand, without attributing it all to the devil (though he is certainly responsible for a lot of suffering). Instead, we must acknowledge that this is the course the human race chose and that the consequences will always be with us to some degree until God restores all things. There is hope and restoration now—it isn't all a "one day" thing—so we embrace redemption and God's blessings as fully as we can. But we also long for the ultimate fulfillment of His Kingdom. It's here, but it isn't fully here. It's okay to live honestly in the tension between those two realities.

The important thing to remember is that, in the grand scope

of God's design, the lament is always momentary and the hope surrounding it is always permanent. No crisis is too big for God, no brokenness beyond His ability to repair, and no sadness too far removed from His restoring touch. In Romans 5:3-5, the apostle Paul urges us to even rejoice in our sufferings, knowing that we are on a certain track toward eternal glory. James and Peter echo the same sentiment, which seems to flow naturally out of the ministry of Jesus. Why does Scripture embrace our laments rather than try to make us snap out of them? Because God's hope becomes real in such times. The sadness of fallen creation becomes the context for God's greatest mercies to be shown. That's worth hanging on to.

The lament is a stop at various stations in life, not a destination. Scripture always leads us out of our sadness—sometimes slowly, but never tentatively. Our hope is certain. God is a restorer. We are called to be people of faith. And the One who calls us will faithfully keep His promises.

## Questions for Reflection

When is a lament spiritually helpful, and when is it a distortion of God's hope? How can we lament appropriately without slipping into harmful negativity?

 DAY 30

# PSALMS 90–106

Though the Psalms are filled with numerous laments, they contain more praises—songs of gratitude and wonder and celebration over who God is and what He has done. For its simplicity and brevity, Psalm 100 is perhaps the best known of these. Like other psalms of praise, it focuses on overflowing gratitude and exuberant worship—attitudes that may seem far removed from the daily experience of most Christians. We don't naturally shout with joy to the Lord or enter His gates with thanksgiving. Yet these are some of the most-often repeated instructions in Scripture. Why? Because He is worthy of shouts of joy and deep gratitude and because we were created to enjoy Him in this way.

This fourth "book" of psalms contains several other well-known passages, including the prayer of Moses (Psalm 90, assumed to be the oldest psalm in Scripture); the "psalm of protection," often quoted by soldiers and anyone else regularly in harm's way (Psalm 91); an ode in which David reminds himself to bless God for all His benefits, which are expressions of His generosity, kindness, and gentle mercy (Psalm 103); and one of several psalms that recite Israel's history as powerful evidence of God's attributes (Psalm 105). In all of these, themes of praise and gratitude come through clearly.

So why don't these attitudes regularly characterize our lives? Perhaps it's because we look at life through the wrong lenses. Trials and hardships loom large in our thinking because we tend to focus on our needs rather than on what has already been fixed. It's human nature, but it's not an accurate perspective. The old metaphor of whether the glass is half empty or half full may be good for distinguishing between pessimists and optimists, but even when our glass is 95 percent full, we still have a tendency to fixate on the 5 percent that's empty. We target the things that aren't right in our lives and allow them to grow to unhealthy dimensions. God calls us back to truth—to an accurate picture of His majesty and glory and His work in us. If we really think about it, His blessings far outweigh our hardships and He is bigger than any of our circumstances. And that's what the praise psalms urge us to do: really think about it.

Something powerful happens inside of us when we worship in

spite of apparent contradictions or deeply felt pain in our lives or when we give thanks even when we don't understand what God is doing through our trials. When we are able to persist in these attitudes, we somehow rise above our circumstances and all the confusion and despair they can burden us with. God steps into those praises, sometimes in subtle ways and sometimes almost palpably. It's more than a psychological boost (though that certainly helps); it's a shift in the spiritual atmosphere of our lives. And if we look carefully, it's usually the catalyst that transforms a psalm that begins in crisis into a psalm that ends in victory. That catalyst becomes a real, transforming aspect of our lives when we can move from despair to triumph even before the battle is fought. Praise and gratitude change the climate and stir up our faith.

That's why we must be vigilant about our thoughts and make sure we fill them with God's glory and goodness. Fallen brains need to be rewired with truth, and worshiping God with gratitude and praise is the best way to do that. Incorporating the Psalms into our prayer lives can have a profound impact, especially when we come to the same conclusions that the psalmists reached: that God is on His throne, that He is passionately involved in the lives of His people, and that regardless of all the ups and downs, this entire adventure begins and ends with glory.

## Questions for Reflection

What happens inside of us when we worship in spite of apparent contradictions in our lives or in the midst of deep pain? Why are joy, gratitude, and praise appropriate in any situation?

DAY 31

# PSALMS 107–150

In all of the Psalms' emotional swings and personal experiences, it's easy to forget that embedded deep within them is a strain of prophecy pointing to the Messiah. We've seen messianic prophecies in the first book of psalms (Psalms 2 and 22), and the fifth book contains the Old Testament verse quoted and/or paraphrased more than any other in the New Testament: "The LORD said to my Lord, 'Sit in the place of honor at my right hand until I humble your enemies, making them a footstool under your feet'" (Psalm 110:1). Clearly, there is some process of profound and decisive victory that God's people will have over His enemies before the Son returns—namely, while He is sitting at the right hand of the Father. Jesus quotes this verse in reference to Himself, and New Testament writers pick up on the theme often. But there are other prophetic verses from the Psalms as well: the Messiah is a priest according to the line of Melchizedek (Psalm 110:4), the stone rejected by the builders becomes the chief cornerstone (Psalm 118:22), and a promise to put a descendant of David's on the throne is reaffirmed (Psalm 132:11). There are plenty of other noteworthy songs and poems scattered throughout the 150 chapters of the Bible's worship book, but significantly, in this heartfelt collection of prayers, the longing for a Redeemer comes to the surface often.

Book Five contains other kinds of psalms as well, including the longest chapter in the Bible, Psalm 119, a thorough meditation on the benefits of God's Word. It also contains a collection of "songs of ascent" (Psalms 120–134), choruses that were most likely sung by pilgrims on their way to Jerusalem to worship at the Temple or participate in Israel's feasts. Psalm 145 (along with a couple of other verses) is recited three times daily in Orthodox

Jewish prayers. And Psalm 150 concludes the book appropriately with one of the highest notes of praise.

This collection touches on the whole range of life, yet it still points to something more. It stirs up our hunger for complete and final victory over sin and death and the enemies of God's Kingdom. It reminds us of God's attributes and His works on our behalf—but only in samplings of who He is. Both the psalmists and their readers knew that life in a fallen world continues until the messianic expectation is completely fulfilled. The rescuer comes at moments of need, and we worship Him at any time, but the complete communion we can have with Him is still reserved for the end of the age.

In Book One, Psalm 16:11 points forward to that time: "You will show me the way of life, granting me the joy of your presence and the pleasures of living with you forever." David hungers and thirsts for that presence throughout his writings, seeking God's face above all else (Psalm 27:4), even though the Temple he refers to doesn't yet exist. The descendants of Korah declare that a single day in God's courts is better than a thousand anywhere else (Psalm 84:10). And the longings continue throughout the rest of the Psalms, throughout the rest of Hebrew Scripture, and to a significant degree, beyond the Messiah's first coming, even to the end of Revelation, where the people of God cry out for Jesus to come quickly. From the earliest pages of the story, God has turned our vision forward to His restoration of all things. The Psalms celebrate the restoration of some things and plead for the restoration of others. We do too. And we can know, according to the prophetic momentum of Scripture, that our longings will be fulfilled.

## QUESTION FOR REFLECTION

In what sense are the messianic prophecies in the Psalms an answer to the needs and desires expressed in each psalm?

DAY 3 2

# PROVERBS

Early in his reign, God gave King Solomon an invitation to ask for anything he wanted. Solomon prudently asked for wisdom, and God gave him that and much more. First Kings and 2 Chronicles tell us how God's response played out in his life—how the king became known far and wide for his wise decisions, as well as for his wealth, building projects, numerous wives, and the glory of his kingdom. The king whose name means "peace" had peace on every side. But he also failed to live up to his own wisdom, forsaking quite a few commands God had given in the Law, being enticed not only by his foreign wives' seductions but also by their gods, and becoming disillusioned toward the end of his life with the futility of all his endeavors. He is a profound enigma—the wisest king making terribly unwise choices and living out his last days with regrets.

But in his prime—in the seasons of his life in which his godly wisdom flourished—he wrote thousands of proverbs and songs (1 Kings 4:32). Many of these have been preserved for us in the book of Proverbs, which also includes wise sayings from a few other sources. The strongest themes in this book are that wisdom is worth seeking more than the finest treasures the world can offer, the beginning of wisdom and knowledge is the fear of the Lord, there are ways that lead to life and others that lead to death, those who follow the ways of life will never regret it, and those who don't are shortsighted fools. Proverbs covers human relationships, how to handle money, the value of working diligently, the importance of sexual purity, and godly characteristics such as faithfulness, patience, perseverance, honor, and integrity. It encourages us to listen to wise advice, to trust in the Lord and not in our own understanding, and to understand that God's world was founded on wisdom that cannot be violated without doing harm to ourselves. These proverbs are a revelation of the fabric of creation and a description of life as it is meant to be lived.

But what are we to make of this advice? Are these laws and commands? Are they hard-and-fast promises? Or are they simply fatherly advice from someone who has seen a lot of life and understands the ways of the world? We know we can't embrace this wisdom too rigidly. For one, God wants us to live in relationship with Him, not in relationship with principles. He doesn't give us an instruction manual and tell us simply to follow the directions. He's much more personal than that. We have to learn how to hear His voice—which, surprisingly to many people, doesn't always apply the same truth to every situation. We see this dynamic clearly in Proverbs, which tells us that if our ways are pleasing to God, even our enemies will be at peace with us (Proverbs 16:7)—although this truth did not seem to apply to Joseph, Moses, David, any of the prophets, any of the disciples, or even Jesus Himself, whose enemies certainly were not at peace with Him.

What do we do when we consider a promise in Scripture and then encounter its exact opposite? For example, how does Proverbs 16:7 mesh with 2 Timothy 3:12: "Everyone who wants to live a godly life in Christ Jesus will suffer persecution"? Or how do we respond when Proverbs 6:6-8 encourages us to save for the future and Jesus urges us not to (Matthew 6:19)? Or when Proverbs tells us that true humility leads to riches, honor, and long life (Proverbs 22:4) and then we read about the martyrdom of Stephen or James? These anomalies create a crisis for those who have weak faith or demand rigid linear logic, but they add to the richness of our conversation with God if we understand them correctly. They are general guidance for how we should normally live, and they are verses that the Spirit of God may illuminate and apply to certain seasons of our lives—in which case they *do* become hard-and-fast promises because He has applied them to us.

But that's the point: We can only understand Proverbs in the context of a genuine, dynamic conversation with God—in the context of a relationship with Him. He will not let us develop a relationship with precepts and apply them across the board, as Job's friends were inclined to do. God's truth and His character aren't relative, of course, but His methods and applications are as varied as our personalities and circumstances. Like any good parent, God understands the individuality, growth phases, strengths and weaknesses, and immediate and long-term needs of each of His children. And His Word is filled with varied revelations of truth that apply to whatever situation we face in whatever season of life we face it. Proverbs is filled with such revelations, and if we stay in conversation with God about them, He will apply them to our lives in the right ways at the right times. That's the essence of wisdom.

## QUESTIONS FOR REFLECTION

Why is it dangerous to view the Proverbs as rigid, unbending principles that are always proven true? In what ways can they (and any other section of Scripture) become a substitute for our relationship with God? How should we apply them to our lives?

 DAY 33

# ECCLESIASTES

The Bible is a book of hope. Ecclesiastes isn't. That contrast has led many to wonder why these musings from the hand of Solomon made it into Scripture. After all, the rest of the Bible builds meaning into our lives, draws us into an eternal relationship with God, and invokes blessing on those who follow Him wholeheartedly.

Ecclesiastes asserts that life is brief, meaningless, and disappointing. There could hardly be a more antithetical message.

But that's part of the beauty of God's revelation to us. It's very textured, for one thing, which greatly stretches those who want a black-and-white world with two-dimensional characters. On top of that, it's brutally honest. The truth is that both perspectives—the eternal hope and the temporal despair—are valid assessments of the human experience. Life "under the sun," as Ecclesiastes puts it, really is futile, frustrating, and disillusioning. From our earthbound point of view, the world ends up offering us nothing lasting or ultimately significant—especially when we invest ourselves in the passing vapors of life that seem so real. But from the view of the rest of God's revelation, everything can have meaning—even our seemingly "meaningless" toil and trials in time and space. Ecclesiastes strips away the eternal perspective and shows us what we have without it. And it isn't a pretty picture.

If anyone could represent that perspective with authority, Solomon could. He was wealthier than anyone around, so he certainly knew what he was talking about when he said money doesn't satisfy. He had more women than any dedicated hedonist could dream of, so he was certainly qualified to say that physical pleasure in itself isn't meaningful. He had vast power over his kingdom and influence in several others, so he knew firsthand that power isn't the key to happiness. He had fame that reached into other nations, but his reputation wasn't enough to prop up his self-esteem in any lasting way. He was a zealous pursuer of knowledge and wisdom, yet even that didn't fulfill his need for significance. This man who had no shortage of gold realized that all that glitters in this world is ultimately pointless. No experience, no pleasure, no accomplishment fulfilled its promises to satisfy him. In themselves, all of these things leave a person empty.

Perhaps that's why God gave Solomon so much and allowed him to experience the futility of it all—so he would become a case study in humanist endeavors and write about it for all the world to see. Such disillusionment—and granted, much of it was self-inflicted by his casual disobedience and even blatant idolatry—sends us searching for the true meaning of life, something that is beyond this under-the-sun existence, something that lasts forever and is truly valuable. In other words, disillusionment sends us in search of a Savior. In that sense, Ecclesiastes is one of the most powerful books in the Bible. Its depression leads us somewhere important.

But even in this existential journey, Ecclesiastes gives us glimpses of true wisdom and shows us some glimmers of hope. This is the book that tells us that our lives have seasons—that there's a time for everything under heaven, a concept that eliminates the pressure to "arrive" at a perfect season of life and stay there. When we grasp the seasons God has ordained—some are fruitful, some aren't; some are happy, some are sad; some are for tearing down, others for building up—we feel much less like failures in the hard times. And we understand, as "the teacher" of Ecclesiastes assures us, that God makes everything beautiful in its time and sets eternity in our hearts (Ecclesiastes 3:11, NIV). Despite futility and disappointments, there *is* hope, there *is* eternity, and there *is* meaning—even in a book that laments the loss of these dreams in the present time.

We need to be careful not to put off all our dreams and fulfillment to the "one day" of the afterlife. The weight of Scripture sides with David in affirming that we will see God's goodness even in the land of the living (Psalm 27:13). But no matter how much of His goodness we see, we will, like Solomon, always long for more. And even in one of Scripture's deepest valleys, we are assured that we will have it.

## QUESTIONS FOR REFLECTION

In what ways does Ecclesiastes point us to Jesus? How is it a reflection of some of the philosophies and lifestyles of our own era?

DAY 34

# SONG OF SONGS

The Song of Songs is filled with powerful images, many of which make us blush. Well, perhaps we don't blush as much as Jews and Christians throughout history have—we've become somewhat desensitized to sexual imagery by its pervasive presence in our society—but we may be startled to find an erotic poem in the pages of the Bible. Surely sex doesn't fit well with our higher spiritual aspirations, does it? Yet God's revelation isn't shy at all about human sexuality, particularly within the context of marriage. In fact, in that light, Scripture celebrates sexuality. Unlike some Greek thought that labeled the spirit as good and the flesh as bad, Hebraic thought embraces God's design for creation. And one of the most beautiful aspects of God's design is human sexuality.

So this song—presumably by Solomon, though his name may appear simply because it was written about him or in his honor—dives deep into a marital relationship. Apparently the couple has just gotten married or is about to be married, and portions of the poem seem to flash back to the time leading up to the wedding. The lyrics revel in sensuality and physical beauty, as well as in the playful give-and-take of a growing intimate relationship. The Song is filled with anticipation, friendships supportive of the relationship, dramatic tension at times of separation, and extravagant expressions of love. Its two most famous passages point to the overwhelming, even intoxicating, power of relentless, passionate love. And they endorse this kind of love as godly.

> He has brought me to his banquet hall,
>     and his banner over me is love.
> SONG OF SONGS 2:4, NASB

Place me like a seal over your heart,
    like a seal on your arm.
For love is as strong as death,
    its jealousy as enduring as the grave.
Love flashes like fire,
    the brightest kind of flame.
Many waters cannot quench love,
    nor can rivers drown it.
If a man tried to buy love
    with all his wealth,
    his offer would be utterly scorned.

SONG OF SONGS 8:6-7

The passion portrayed in the Song is so powerful that many throughout history, both Jewish and Christian, have interpreted it as an allegory of God's love. Some have done so in far too much detail, forcing every word or verse into a picture of the divine/human relationship. That doesn't work very well, but the broader, big picture application does. This love is literally called "the very flame of the LORD" (Song of Solomon 8:6, ESV, NASB). In light of the fact that Jeremiah 2:2 and rabbinic tradition have considered God's meeting with Israel at Mount Sinai a betrothal ceremony; that the prophets considered Israel's unfaithfulness not only as disobedience but as *adultery*; that God inspired Hosea to demonstrate God's faithfulness in terms of a husband with an unfaithful wife; that Jesus referred to Himself as a bridegroom; that Paul used the marriage metaphor to describe Christ and the church; and that Revelation ends with a wedding, we can safely say that the Song is an appropriate portrayal of God's love for His people. It isn't only that—the ode to sexual love in marriage is its primary purpose—but the poem's language and its place in the divine story point to a bigger picture. Human beings love this passionately because

God loves this passionately. Those made in His image had to get it from somewhere. This depth of love has a divine source and is experienced by the divine heart.

This truth has huge implications for those who belong to God. We are not just His servants, the sheep in His pasture, or the clay vessels made by the Master Potter. His desire for intimacy goes much deeper than that. This is the driving passion behind creation and redemption, as evidenced by the enormous cost God paid in order to reestablish the union we lost in Eden. An infinite heart has infinite love—intense, relentless, unquenchable—and it stops at nothing until its desire is fulfilled. As the objects of this love's desire, that's our response too—to stop at nothing until it is fulfilled. God pursues us until we place Him as a seal upon our hearts. And our relationship with Him takes on deeper, more ultimately fulfilling dimensions.

## QUESTIONS FOR REFLECTION

As an expression of marital sex and pleasure, what does the Song reveal about God and His personality? As an allegory of our relationship with God, what does the Song say about Him?

 DAY 35

# ISAIAH 1–39

God speaks. That should come as no surprise—the existence of the Bible itself is enough to convince most Christians that our God is vocal—but some still wonder if He speaks directly to people about specific events and situations. The fact that the Bible is full of prophetic voices reveals His desire to express Himself to His people. He created us for relationship, and relationships are nothing without active, ongoing communication. When people need to hear the voice of their Father, He speaks.

Not only is Isaiah the first of the prophetic books in the Christian canon, it is also considered the prototype of this genre of literature. Isaiah is a far-reaching book, covering not only a particular time in history, but also a huge portion of Israel's existence as a nation and the distant future of God's Kingdom. Isaiah is quoted in the New Testament more than any other Old Testament prophet. In some ways, his book functions as a Bible within the Bible; even its structure reflects the whole of Scripture, with thirty-nine chapters of judgment and prophecy devoted to Israel, its role in God's plan, and the historical/political landscape around His people (corresponding to the thirty-nine books of the Old Testament) and twenty-seven chapters of messianic foreshadowing, predictions of salvation, and pictures of new heavens and a new earth (corresponding to the twenty-seven books of the New Testament). Its prophecies pick up on nearly every theme of God's fuller revelation.

Many of Isaiah's prophecies seem to be running on parallel tracks—one track addressing the immediate or near-future concerns of the original audience and the other pointing to a greater cosmic picture on a grander scale. That's because the language is at times directly relevant and at other times—often in the same passage—well beyond the scope of that era of history or even the realm of time and space. For example, in Isaiah 7, a passage dominated by talk of Assyria and Egypt, two powers between whom Israel and Judah were uncomfortably wedged, the prophet speaks of a child to be born. A virgin (or a young woman) will conceive, and before the child is old enough to know right from wrong, the Assyrian threat will be rendered impotent. At first glance, this is a sign for the current king of Judah, not for a Roman-dominated province some seven centuries later. Yet this child will be called

Immanuel, "God with us"—a name the New Testament writers apply to Jesus. In Isaiah 9:6, we're told of a child who will be called Mighty God and Everlasting Father—two terms that simply cannot apply to any Jewish boy of Isaiah's day. This immediate *and* future dynamic in prophecy is the subject of heated theological debates, but it's the nature of God's Word. He speaks, and His voice often has multiple applications, sometimes echoing its purposes throughout the millennia to come. In chapter 14, is Isaiah speaking of the king of Babylon or of a once-beautiful archangel with deity envy? The answer may well be *both*. In chapter 7, is the young woman who will conceive a child the prophet's wife or a Galilean virgin hundreds of years later? Apparently God's Word not only doesn't return to Him empty, it returns with multiple fulfillments, just like seed sown into the ground and watered (Isaiah 55:10-11). The harvest of true prophecy is plentiful.

Such is the case with Isaiah's calling as well. In chapter 6, he goes to the Temple to worship and encounters God, high and lifted up. Struck by his own sin and then cleansed of it, he is given an assignment to warn people who will not hear. Jesus applies these words to Himself—with added emphasis that He preaches in such a way that the rebellious *cannot* hear (Matthew 13:14-15). This prophecy is certainly fulfilled in Isaiah's time, but also in Jesus' time. So is the prophecy of Israel as God's vineyard (Isaiah 5), a powerful image taken to heart by God's people throughout history, yet one that Jesus applies to Himself as the true Israel (i.e., the "true vine" of John 15:1). Even in these often hard-to-swallow chapters, there are glimpses of future and ultimate fulfillment.

This is how God's Word resonates in our lives too. There are immediate applications and promises fulfilled, as well as greater applications and greater fulfillments as we grow deeper and stronger in His Kingdom. We get foretastes of glory now and much greater gulps of it later. We see the seeds of the Kingdom growing in our lives and in our period of history, knowing that an even fuller experience of it is coming. Why? Because God speaks to His people, and His words never die. They simply bear bigger and better fruit as time goes by.

## QUESTIONS FOR REFLECTION

In what ways does the book of Isaiah reflect the Bible as a whole? Why is it quoted so often in the New Testament?

 DAY 36

# ISAIAH 40–59

Though there are certainly moments of victory and encouragement in the first thirty-nine chapters of Isaiah, for the most part they are pretty rough on God's people. But chapter 40 opens with an announcement of comfort. The shift—not only in substance and mood but also in style and in the time period covered—is so sudden that many consider this section of Isaiah a later addition by another Isaiah-like author. It speaks of the end of judgment, the time when Judah's captivity is completed and Jews can return to their homeland and rebuild. They will go out with joy and be led in peace, as the mountains and hills break forth in song. According to the prophet, a time of celebration is coming.

Yet this portion of Isaiah's prophecy has several themes in common with the previous section. God emphasizes again and again that He is the only true God and there is no other. He alone is worthy of worship, and He still draws His people into a heart-to-heart relationship with Himself. He alone is sovereign over the maneuvers of nations and kings and over the lives of ordinary people. He alone can see into the future and discern the end of a matter even from the very beginning. And from that perspective—high above all powers on earth, high above human thoughts and ways—He can assure His people that His plans are good and that they have a future worth hoping for. Regardless of how things look now, the promise of the Kingdom is better.

Toward that end, deliverers are coming. Cyrus of Persia is anointed by God to release the captives of Babylon. Israel itself has a role as God's instrument for the nations, a "suffering servant" called into a unique place of redemption in history. But this servant figure—one that shows up in at least four passages of Isaiah—can't refer only to Israel. The servant is specifically identified as Israel in Isaiah 49:3, for example, yet ministers to Israel as its restorer only two verses later. As in other prophetic declarations, multiple levels and applications are at work; words that apply to a nation are mixed with words that apply to an individual, and language that can only apply to the present is interwoven with language that can only apply to the distant future. And with the portrayal of the servant in chapter 53, it's virtually impossible *not* to connect this mysterious figure with the crucified Messiah portrayed in the New Testament. The description is too accurate to be coincidental.

This section of Isaiah urges a return to the covenant—for God's people to look back to the quarry from which they were taken (Abraham's faith and covenant with God); to turn their hearts away from idols and back to the God who loves them; and to experience His truth at a deeply heartfelt level, observing fasts not of ritual, but of justice and compassion. Yet human beings can't simply improve their own condition—one reason Israel's servant-hood must be supplemented by a fully righteous servant sent by God Himself. Sin has separated the people from God. He looks for a human being to intercede and finds none, so He determines to provide His own solution. He will accomplish salvation Himself.

Even though the dominant theme of the first section of Isaiah is judgment, the dominant theme of the second is hope. These are songs of deliverance. The barren ones will sing in celebration over their fruitfulness, tents will be enlarged, the thirsty can come and drink water, wine, and milk at no cost. God's people are engraved on the palms of His hands; He simply cannot forsake them, even when He has chastised them harshly. He will become the husband and redeemer of His people. Though He abandoned them for a moment, He will bring them back with deep and everlasting compassion. His commitment to His covenant and His beloved is unbreakable.

That's why Isaiah is such a reassuring book to so many. We need the comfort of a God who overcomes our shortcomings and fills us with hope in spite of them. When life feels threatening and overwhelming, we need to know that God already knows the end of our circumstances and can assure us that everything will work together for good. And after all our attempts to deliver ourselves, we need the promise of a deliverer. We need to be rescued—from situations, from futility, even from ourselves. Isaiah points us in that direction with words that ring true again and again.

## Questions for Reflection

What do Isaiah's predictions of restoration and of the Messiah tell us about God's sovereignty over history? How do they serve as evidence of who Jesus is? In what ways is the hope of these chapters relevant to your current needs and circumstances?

 DAY 37

# ISAIAH 60–66

God's people are to arise and shine. Why? Their light has come, and the glory of the Lord has risen upon them. Clearly these words were future-oriented when Isaiah wrote them, even though they are in the present tense: There is a time when thick darkness will cover the earth and God's people will shine. It can't be when Jesus returns—thick darkness covering the earth does not describe His Kingdom. It has to be before then. In other words, those who have experienced the Lord's glory are called to shine in such a way that nations come to their light (Isaiah 60:1-3).

This is how the last section of Isaiah begins. These last seven chapters contain pictures of final judgment as well as pictures of ultimate salvation. At the synagogue in Nazareth, Jesus applies a quote from chapter 61 to His ministry—the Spirit of the Lord is upon Him to bring good news to the poor, give freedom to captives, and declare God's favor (Luke 4:18-19). But He stops quoting in the middle of a sentence, right before declaring the day of God's vengeance. That theme of judgment isn't part of His advent; it's a characteristic of the Second Coming. In the meantime, the nations will see the righteousness of God, and Zion's righteousness will go forth as a blazing torch. God will delight over His people as a bridegroom delights over his bride. The words of the prophet express humanity's longing for this redeeming God to come down and dwell with His people.

That day is coming. It has already come, in some sense; the Spirit of God already dwells with human beings. But Isaiah pictures new heavens and a new earth that have not yet come. When they do, the former things will not be remembered. Those who die at one hundred years of age will be considered short-lived. Wolves and lambs will lie down together. All labor will be fruitful. In that era, God will answer His people even before they call to Him. All the toil, all the frustration, all the angst of being God's chosen will be worth it. All flesh—or at least all who have not rebelled against Him and suffered His judgment—will rejoice with Jerusalem, worship God, and experience His peace.

Nowhere in Hebrew Scripture is God's desire to draw nations

to Himself clearer than in Isaiah. There are other places that demonstrate His intention to establish His Kingdom on earth—His commission in Eden to subdue the earth, His scattering of the people at Babel, His drawing of Gentiles to worship at the Temple in Jerusalem, for example—but this is the most apparent. His desire is for all peoples, all languages and cultures, all ethnicities to worship Him. Israel was chosen as the firstborn of many nations, a priest-nation representing God to others. Restoration is God's goal for this planet, and it's all-inclusive.

That should encourage us. Many have spiritualized the gospel so thoroughly that we can't envision it affecting actual nations and cultures in time and space. We perceive it as a one-day, other-worldly promise. But Isaiah and the rest of Scripture bring the Kingdom to earth in real time for real people to experience. Yes, there are mysteries about when and how it will manifest—the Bible doesn't tie up all our loose ends for us. But there are solid hints that God is building His Kingdom even now through His people *and* that the glory of God shines through His people before the Messiah comes again.

So the question becomes, how do we shine? How do we reflect the glory of a God with such a comprehensive cosmic agenda? What role do we play in His Kingdom? Isaiah has given us plenty of clues: God pursues wholehearted worship and grieves when we give ourselves to less worthy loves; He wants us to express His justice and compassion; and He wants us to be filled with faith and hope about His purposes for this world. At any moment in any place, we can be confident that God wants us to align ourselves with His character and His Kingdom—not simply to look forward to them one day, but to embody them now. He defends and supports those who are His people not only in name but also in practice. When our mission lines up with His, His Kingdom is revealed.

## QUESTIONS FOR REFLECTION

What role do we play in God's coming Kingdom? In what ways can we "arise" and "shine" with God's glory on us? What do you think God means by "new heavens and a new earth" in Isaiah 65:17?

 DAY 38

# JEREMIAH 1–29

Many people believe that obeying God completely will always bring a sense of fulfillment and peace. The book of Jeremiah refutes that misperception. Throughout this book, the prophet does exactly what God calls him to do, yet his lament in chapter 20 sums up his experience well: "O Lord, you misled me. . . . His word burns in my heart like a fire. It's like a fire in my bones! I am worn out trying to hold it in! I can't do it! . . . I curse the day I was born! . . . My entire life has been filled with trouble, sorrow, and shame" (Jeremiah 20:7, 9, 14, 18). His honesty is refreshing and acceptable to God, but it's nonetheless excruciating.

.This is God's assignment for Jeremiah: to grieve over Jerusalem. Why? Because biblical prophets normally weren't called to simply deliver a message. They were called to *embody* God's message. Jeremiah's mission in life is to represent God's heart—the grief and pain of the Creator over the disobedience of His people and the devastation coming upon them. Jeremiah was chosen even before he was born to be a picture of God's pain, and he is very successful at it.

This longest of the prophetic books is not designed to bring the nation to repentance. The benefits of repentance are offered, of course, but both God and Jeremiah know that the people won't turn around. They have too many other "prophets" giving them false messages of assurance, and they are too blind to the evil of their sins, which include idolatry (at times involving child sacrifices), injustice, ignoring the Sabbath, violence, and dishonesty. Some pagan practices have even been brought into the Temple. Jeremiah is the last major prophet to preach before Judah's captivity in Babylon—he is in Jerusalem before, during, and after Babylon's two major sieges against the city—and his message is so harsh because things have gotten so bad. Jeremiah is not to intercede for the nation because God has already said He won't listen. Judah is like a flawed vessel on the potter's wheel, and its potter is determined to reshape it. The prophecies are simply to prepare the people for judgment and to serve as a record that God had tried to reach them. Judah will know the truth of Jeremiah's words when it's already too late. But at least they will know.

So Jeremiah must endure painful experiences such as imprisonment, being confined in a cistern, a plot to kill him (orchestrated by men of his hometown, perhaps including some of his own brothers), isolation, the burning of his messages (which had to be completely rewritten), and severe depression and emotional pain. He is called "the weeping prophet" for a reason.

Yet in spite of the catastrophe coming upon Jerusalem, God still knows the plans He has for His people—plans for good and not for evil, to give them a hope and a future. His judgment is not for the sake of destroying but for the sake of restoring. This captivity will last only seventy years—a prophecy that becomes very significant later as Daniel reads Jeremiah's scroll. After that, God will bring many of His people back to their homeland.

One of the striking things about Jeremiah's prophecies is that the choices of human beings have the capacity to cause God to feel pain. Our theology tends to place God above the swell of emotions, but His Word doesn't. These are the declarations not of a capricious deity who has been offended but of a husband who has been betrayed (see Jeremiah 2:2; 3:6-10). The spiritual condition of God's people is described as adultery. The God who hates divorce threatens to divorce His people. Yes, He relents and restores the relationship, but the betrayal and the wounds are real. We'll see this theme again in the books of Ezekiel and Hosea, among others. God can have a broken heart.

That tells us a lot about His desire for us. He wants not just a friendship but an intimate relationship. If He feels pain and grief from our choices to love others more than we love Him, then He certainly feels joy when we choose to love Him. Few people realize what an astounding invitation that is, and even fewer accept the invitation. But those who do can experience God in remarkable ways.

## QUESTIONS FOR REFLECTION

Why is the mission to represent God's heart not always a pleasant one? Why didn't God give Jeremiah a more fulfilling task? Does the picture of God grieving and feeling pain change your perception of Him? Why or why not?

 DAY 39

# JEREMIAH 30-52

As the prophets tended to do, Jeremiah acts out many of his predictions for God's people. He places a basket of good figs and a basket of bad figs in front of the Temple—the good representing those who have already been taken into exile (and are therefore being reshaped by God) and the bad representing the undisciplined and unrepentant ones who remain in Jerusalem. He buries a linen garment near the Euphrates River and then digs it up, picturing the uselessness of sinful people who have left their God. He cuts off his hair as a sign of rejection, is told by God not to marry and have children, and wears a symbolic yoke on his neck as he walks around the city. Now he is told to buy a piece of land in a Babylonian-occupied area outside Jerusalem—even while telling the captives already in Babylon to build houses and settle down because they are going to be there a while. This land purchase makes a statement that even though the captivity is devastating and real, it isn't permanent. God has instructed the prophet to go ahead and make plans for the people's return.

This purchase comes in the "book of consolations" (Jeremiah 30–33), a hope-filled section of an otherwise dreadful prophecy. God is with His people, and a new Exodus is coming after the Exile. He has loved them with an everlasting love and drawn them to Himself with unfailing faithfulness. And not only will He bring them back to the land, but He will establish a new covenant and put within them a new heart. They will all know Him directly— not through priests or hearsay.

This is the same message found in the New Testament. That message is scattered throughout Hebrew Scripture long before its fulfillment in the Gospels and Acts. God isn't interested in simply reforming our behavior or giving us a set of principles and precepts to follow. His agenda goes much deeper than that. If Scripture has shown us anything up to this point, it's that fallen human nature will inevitably fail to connect with God. The only way we can be restored is to be fundamentally changed.

That's why we have to be born into a new kind of life and God's Spirit must be implanted within us. Hearing truth and try-ing to carry it out is ultimately futile, something akin to a cat trying to become a dog simply by barking. It isn't possible, and even if it were, it wouldn't fool anyone. A real transformation must happen within our hearts, and that change will inevitably work its way outward. Under this new covenant, with this new heart, God's people won't love others because they are told to; they will love because they are loving. They won't display God's character through self-discipline; they will display His character because they will actually have it. The New Covenant, when rightly applied and experienced, changes us at the core.

Sadly, Jeremiah is only able to point to this promise of the new heart; it won't be realized for some time. After the destruction of Jerusalem and the devastation of the Temple, the prophet is carried off to Egypt with escapees whom he warned against trying to flee to Egypt. But God's lengthy, yet thorough, plan of restoring His creation presses ahead, with all its pain and perseverance. He will be relentless in carrying it out, or as another prophet declared, the zeal of the Lord will accomplish it. The God of the new heart knew from before the Fall that this was where He was headed with these people who bear His image. They will become like Him and relate to Him at astonishing spiritual depths. And there will be no need for harsh, devastating judgments anymore. They will become one with Him.

## QUESTION FOR REFLECTION

Why is a new heart necessary for us to love and follow God?

 DAY 40

# LAMENTATIONS

The weeping prophet has never wept more than he does when Jerusalem falls. He has prophesied through two invasions of the city, during which many of its inhabitants (including Ezekiel and Daniel) have been taken back to Babylon as captives. But this siege is the worst. It leaves the city in ruins; the Temple—God's own dwelling place—is now rubble. The chosen people seem to be utterly forsaken. The plan of God seems to be completely abandoned. Darkness has truly overcome the world.

The destruction of Jerusalem is a rebuke to all who assumed that God would never bring shame on His own people and, by implication, on His own name. The people can hardly believe that God would take His anger this far. "O LORD, think about this! Should you treat your own people this way? Should mothers eat their own children, those they once bounced on their knees? Should priests and prophets be killed within the Lord's Temple?" (Lamentations 2:20). The prophet is filled with bitterness as he walks through the city and sees smoldering ruins and children lying dead in the streets. This is the unthinkable outcome, the ancient equivalent of nuclear destruction. Jeremiah must face the prospect of living in what we would describe as a postapocalyptic world. Words can hardly portray the sense of loss he must feel.

Yet even in the midst of hopelessness, Jeremiah interrupts his graphic lament with a bigger truth:

> The thought of my suffering and homelessness
> > is bitter beyond words.
> I will never forget this awful time,
> > as I grieve over my loss.
> Yet I still dare to hope
> > when I remember this:

> The faithful love of the LORD never ends!
> > His mercies never cease.
> Great is his faithfulness;
> > his mercies begin afresh each morning.
> I say to myself, "The LORD is my inheritance;
> > therefore, I will hope in him!"

The LORD is good to those who depend on him,
 to those who search for him.
So it is good to wait quietly
 for salvation from the LORD.

LAMENTATIONS 3:19-26

The contrast between despair and hope—and the force of will required to adopt hope in life's bleakest moments—makes a profound statement about how we are to walk through this world. When we are faced with visible contradictions to our faith, with what appears to be evidence that God isn't good or that His promises aren't true after all, we have a choice to make. We can trust our own vision and lean on our own understanding, or we can decide that God is who He says He is regardless of what we see and understand. Jeremiah does the latter. He knows God's people have rebelled and that His severe judgment against them is warranted, but he also knows that God does not abandon His purposes or the compassionate nature of His own heart. Jeremiah seems to understand that the sprawling devastation in front of him is not the end of the story.

Whatever trials we go through today aren't the end of the story either. It can be tempting to judge God in the middle of the story, but all good stories have moments when all seems lost. It's the ending that makes it good—the overcoming of impossible odds and ominous threats with heroic deeds, great victories, and final redemption. This is where God's story is headed, both on a global scale and at a very personal level in each of our lives. The ending will prove that the devastating setbacks and dilemmas of the journey were worthwhile.

So we can say with Jeremiah that God's mercies are new every morning and that His faithfulness is great. Because of His great love, we never need to lose heart. In fact, we can have hope even in the midst of our greatest crises. Those crises are always temporary, but God's deliverance is eternal. The middle of the story is only for a moment.

## QUESTIONS FOR REFLECTION

Why do you think God had Jeremiah preach when He knew His people wouldn't listen? In the midst of our hardest times, worst failures, and deepest pain, why is it important to remember that God's mercies are new every morning? How can we experience His new mercies?

 DAY 41

# EZEKIEL 1–39

While Jeremiah has been warning Jerusalem of its impending fall, Ezekiel prophesies to the exiles who have already been taken to Babylon. Many of them understand that God has judged, but they believe they have seen the extent of His judgment. But the Holy City and its holy Temple will become rubble. Nevertheless, in spite of all appearances, God has not abandoned His people. Without a powerful prophetic voice, the exiles in a faraway land will not be able to make sense of these seemingly contradictory statements. Ezekiel is that voice.

Perhaps more than with any other prophet, Ezekiel's message is visual. God speaks in pictures more than He speaks in words—some prophets have to "look" to see what God is saying—and that's certainly true in the life of Ezekiel. The prophet has a dramatic vision of God, involving multifaced, multiwinged creatures and wheels within wheels, and then acts out most of his prophecies. He makes a model of Jerusalem and lays siege to it; he lies on his side for more than four hundred days to portray the years of sin committed by Israel and Judah; he cooks his food over dung to show how God's people must now eat defiled food among the nations; he cuts his hair and divides it into groups—for burning, cutting, scattering, and preserving—to demonstrate how God is chastising His people but preserving a remnant. He also tells very graphic parables about how God rescued Israel when she was a baby, raised her to be a young woman, married her, and then had to put up with her obscene acts of adultery and prostitution (chapter 16). Judah's "watchman" is led by God to make his points with powerful and provocative illustrations.

One of the more lasting and encouraging illustrations from Ezekiel is his vision of restoration in chapter 37. In the vision, God takes him to a valley filled with dry bones—not recently dead bodies, not decaying flesh, but thoroughly dead and disconnected skeletons. God tells him to speak to the bones, and they reconnect and grow flesh. God tells him to speak to the breath—the life, the Spirit—which then comes and breathes life into the bodies. And reminiscent of the way God breathed life into dust in Eden, these once-dry bones become living human beings and stand up to form a vast army. The judged, chastised, destroyed nation will have life in it once again—just as dead souls in sin, dead bodies in a grave, or deathly circumstances in our lives are never beyond God's redemptive work. He can breathe life into anyone or anything.

Pictures like these speak not only to the original audience of Scripture, but to multiple situations and people throughout history as well. They become symbols of victory and hope, reminders that this is who God is—a breather of life, a restorer of whatever has been lost, a victor over death and all lesser enemies. Visuals have multiple applications and a very long shelf life in our minds. This is why Jesus spoke in parables and why God gave us a collection of stories about people who encountered Him rather than a theology textbook composed of doctrinal statements. The Bible is a string of powerful images, not a dissertation on God. Why? Because God's favorite language is pictures.

That's true in our lives too. He teaches us through parables of the seasons in our lives; shows us metaphors in movies, books, and real-life circumstances; displays His glory rather than simply telling us about it; and draws us into truth and to Himself through events and relationships. That means that if we really want to "hear" His voice, we must keep our eyes open, not just our ears. He will very often show us what He is doing in our lives—correcting us, encouraging us, filling us with hope, and promising us a glorious future.

## QUESTIONS FOR REFLECTION

How does the image of God breathing life into dry bones to re-create His people reveal His message more powerfully than simply telling us He is a restorer? Has God used visual illustrations of His truth in your life? If so, how have they affected you?

 DAY 42

# EZEKIEL 40–48

Like Jeremiah, Ezekiel has prophesied of a new creation, a time when God will put a new heart into His people. In the place of corrupt and misleading shepherds, God Himself will be the true Shepherd, rescue His sheep, and tend them with justice and compassion. Now, in the closing chapters of the book, Ezekiel—a priest whose life once centered on the Temple—reveals what a new Jerusalem, a new Temple, and a new experience of God's ongoing presence would look like. And the view is idyllic.

That's because in prophesying of a restored Jerusalem, Ezekiel's language grows bigger and deeper to invoke images of a restored creation. On the surface, this prophecy may be about God's plan to bring His people back from captivity and restore Israel as a nation, but the literal interpretation gives way to ultimate overtones. In contrast to Ezekiel's earlier vision of God withdrawing His presence from the old Temple, this vision shows God increasingly filling the new Temple—which, along with the new Jerusalem, happens to have perfect and rather large dimensions. A rising river portrays God's river of life that is nourishing enough to make even the Dead Sea a welcome habitat for fish. The land is perfectly apportioned among the tribes, the Temple remains perfectly pure and undefiled as the priests preside over the nation's offerings, and the Sabbaths and feasts are observed without fail. This is what God's people are supposed to look like. This is life in the presence of God and in a land filled with His glory.

Jesus and the New Testament writers pick up these images and apply them even more broadly. The river of living water flows from Jesus, who is the Good Shepherd God has promised to the world. The Spirit who falls on the Day of Pentecost fulfills the promise of the new heart. And the presence of God among His people is fulfilled not only in the resurrection of Christ and the indwelling of the Spirit, but also at the end of the age when evil is defeated. Revelation describes the river coming from the throne of God in a land that is so radiant with His glory that there is no longer any night. This is the ultimate restoration, far beyond bringing captives back from Babylon. This restoration brings captives of the human condition back into God's original purpose: an intimate relationship with Him in a place undisturbed by evil. The Garden of Eden becomes the city of God, with the Temple of His presence at the very center. This is where creation is headed.

Sadly, many of the exiles of Ezekiel's time (as well as many people today) placed their hope in that far-off-in-the-future vision and forgot that it has profound immediate implications. If it's God's purpose to establish His Kingdom, fill His people with His presence, and implement justice and compassion throughout the land, it's on His heart *now*. It's absolutely inconceivable that He would say, "We'll deal with all that at the end of the age. Let's just keep the character and the blessings of My Kingdom on hold until then." If God's desire is to shine throughout the world and for His river of life to rise, then His people need not wait to become reflections of His Kingdom in society. We are not just travelers on a long, hard road to our destination. We carry evidence of that destination within us. Whenever God's presence fills us to overflowing, we bring glimpses of the destination into the journey itself. Wherever we see something that doesn't look like the Kingdom, we're to bring the Kingdom into that place. Though in one sense the Kingdom will come, in another sense it has already come and still comes— not just *to* us but *through* us. The builder of the city isn't waiting for "someday." He's working even now.

We see the present reality of the coming future Kingdom throughout the rest of Scripture as well. After the captivity, Jerusalem is rebuilt. Judaism is restored. A Messiah comes, and the new creation is born. The world begins to be transformed. Individuals, families, cities, and nations are affected. Societies are touched with the salt and light and leaven of God's Kingdom. So we can see where this is headed. Those who embrace the vision are blessed by seeing it come to pass in their lives.

## QUESTIONS FOR REFLECTION

What aspects of God's restoration process for His creation can only be accomplished by Him? What aspects can we participate in now?

DAY 43

# DANIEL 1–6

Daniel spends a night in a lions' den and survives. In a sense, he spends several decades in a lions' den and remains faithful. He and several of his friends are some of the early exiles taken to Babylon, probably as young teenagers. The palace's reeducation program puts these young men through at least three years of studies to teach them the language, culture, and religion of their new home. Their names are changed to honor Babylonian deities, and most likely they are made eunuchs. Daniel and his friends become court-officials-in-training—promising young Jews forced to integrate into Babylonian society.

How Daniel and his friends handle this uncomfortable position becomes a case study in living for God in an ungodly world. They are faithful to their superiors in every way possible, but not when faithfulness to their duties compromises their faith in God. They honor pagan authority, but not when they are ordered to eat nonkosher food or bow down to an idol. In some cases, they are allowed exceptions—such as when their Jewish diet proves to be better than the palace diet and they grow stronger. In other cases— such as when Shadrach, Meshach, and Abednego refuse to bow to Nebuchadnezzar's statue and are cast into a fiery furnace, or when Daniel's prayer habits land him in a lions' den—their faithfulness to God and submission to Babylon's punishment results in the vindication of their beliefs. In contrast to other martyrs in Scripture, they don't have to die for their faith; instead, they are elevated to greater esteem and responsibility by the crises their faith creates. They are examples of how God can preserve those who remain uncompromising under extreme social and legal pressure.

Daniel first stands out when Nebuchadnezzar has a dream,

and suspicious that his sages will tell him only what he wants to hear, the king demands—with a threat of execution—that they discern not only the interpretation but also the dream itself. The entire community of advisers—magicians, astrologers, diviners—is thrown into a panic by this ultimatum, but Daniel and his friends know that there's a God in heaven who knows all things and reveals mysteries to His people. They pray, Daniel receives revelation about the dream and its massive political ramifications, and his interpretation spares the realm from the actions of a rash king.

What we find, both from this dream and the rest of Daniel's prophecies, is that God is sovereign over nations, both in ancient times and today. He never panics when empires fall or evil men rule. He isn't thrown by budget crises or dishonest leaders or madmen with their fingers on the controls of weapons of mass destruction. He knows all things in advance, He has a plan, and His plan cannot be thwarted. Yes, evil occurs, but it isn't out of control. There are limits. God has already accounted for every empire that will ever rule and has woven them into His plan. Even if the process is difficult, His people can rest secure in the final outcome.

We also find that God shares His secrets with those who love Him and are faithful to Him. He is not, nor has He ever been, a silent God. Daniel heard God's solution for several national crises and was able to confidently declare truth in the midst of them. While political strategists, cultural commentators, financial analysts, and scientific researchers put their minds to work on society's most intractable problems, sometimes God's people can simply pray for solutions and receive them as revelation, often as a bright idea that comes "out of the blue." That's because God loves to impart truth, but can only do so to those whose eyes and ears are open to it. In other words, Daniel doesn't have to be the exception. The God who reveals secrets has many servants. When we ask Him to speak to us, committing to follow whatever He says, He will make His wisdom known.

## QUESTIONS FOR REFLECTION

How can we know when it's okay to adapt to our culture and when we should remain uncompromising? What does Daniel's example teach us about standing firm for what we believe? Do you believe Daniel's ability to hear God and receive His wisdom is an example for us or an exception that we can't follow? Why?

 DAY 44

# DANIEL 7–12

Every so often, Scripture peels back the veil and shows us a glimpse of what's really going on behind the scenes. The last six chapters of Daniel contain several visions that peer into that realm and give us a divine lens for viewing earthly affairs. The succession of empires that is coming upon the world—Babylon followed by Media and Persia, then by Greece, and finally by Rome—is not an accident of human history. Kingdoms have a higher Judge, and humans can look to a higher King than any earthly authority. In the midst of these political shifts is the Son of Man, who has greater, more lasting dominion than any empire the world has ever seen.

This is good to know when earthly authorities seem threatening, overwhelmingly powerful, and permanent. Empires are merely brief attempts at power that swell and recede like the tide. They may seem to have a handle on human affairs, but they are subject to powers much greater than their leaders can imagine. The true empire—the Kingdom that will come in the midst of all others and eventually supersede all others—may seem insignificant to the kings of this world, but the Ancient of Days is above them all. Daniel is practically paralyzed with awe by His visions of God.

Sometime during his series of visions, Daniel reads in Jeremiah's writings that the sovereign God has decreed that the captivity should last only seventy years. Though many might rest in that fact and wait for God to "do His thing," Daniel is prompted instead to fast, pray with great intensity, and confess the sins of the people. He realizes that God's will isn't accomplished fatalistically. God generally requires the involvement of a human agent—someone to ask, to intercede, to partner with Him in carrying out His work. Just as God's declarations prompted Abraham, Joseph, Moses, David, and others to intercede, here they prompt Daniel to pray as well. God has declared His purpose; it's now up to a human being to pray for it to come to pass.

We rarely approach prophecy the same way Daniel did. For example, Daniel seems to declare things not only about the end of his era but also about the end of human history, yet many biblical speculators simply chart the timelines and watch for things to unfold. Seldom do Christians see themselves as active and necessary participants in the unfolding of prophecy. Only occasionally do we see prophecies as a call to pray that the thing prophesied will come to pass. And when we do pray for what God has declared, we often do so without the intensity and perseverance of Daniel. At one point, Daniel is told that his deep, impassioned prayer had been heard in heaven, but the heavenly agents answering it were resisted in battle for twenty-one days. We get the impression that without Daniel's perseverance, the battle would have been lost or the answer might have been compromised. Daniel's glimpses behind the veil remind us that there is more going on in the world than meets the eye; that cosmic history is at stake; and that even though God is sovereign and will absolutely accomplish His purposes, He will almost always raise up human participants to request the fulfillment of those purposes and shape how they play out. There is no greater privilege than to be one of those human participants.

Daniel's prophecies prompt the question: "What's going on behind the veil of our own lives?" The rest of Scripture assures us that not only is the Ancient One sovereign over geopolitics, He's also sovereign over individuals. He has purposes for our lives, and He calls us to step into them. Only as we draw near to Him—listening for His voice, seeking His vision, and praying for the fulfillment of His plan—do we become active participants in a bigger story than we could ever imagine.

## QUESTIONS FOR REFLECTION

Why do you think Daniel prayed and fasted when he learned of Jeremiah's prophecy that the captivity would last for only seventy years? Do you tend to see God's promises as inevitable, or do you think we are supposed to pray for their fulfillment and receive them by faith? Why?

 DAY 45

# HOSEA

The God of Israel calls for single-minded, wholehearted devotion—worshipers who have affection for Him alone above all other gods. God often speaks of His relationship to His people as a betrothal; the ones He has rescued are His bride. This is to be a deeply personal, intimate union. Yet many in Israel go instead to the temple of Baal, appeal to this storm god for rain and fertile crops, and act out their fertility pleas by engaging with temple prostitutes. Instead of looking to the true God for provision, they bow to a Canaanite idol that also happens to appeal to their baser desires. In terms of the cosmic marriage, they commit adultery.

Several prophets frame Israel's idolatry in terms of the marriage contract, calling it adultery. But Hosea is called to embody the metaphor and act it out. He is told to marry an unfaithful woman named Gomer, who will repeatedly prostitute herself to other lovers. She will bear children—Hosea must wonder whether they are his own or not—who are given pointed prophetic names, and she will be largely indifferent to them. Yet Hosea must remain a faithful husband and a good father. In spite of Gomer's lewd and blatant unfaithfulness, Hosea remains steadfast in the relationship, calling her back to himself, even buying her back when she has sold herself. The prophet's life becomes the prophecy, a picture of God's relationship with His people.

Hosea prophesies at a time when the powerful Assyrians to the north threaten the land. God's people are vulnerable to attack. They are victims of frequent raids and live with the constant danger of being defeated and taken captive. Hosea suggests that this position of vulnerability and the frequent conflicts with Assyria are God's judgment against Israel for her adultery against Him. If they will turn, He will forgive—and protect.

Yet the primary message of Hosea isn't judgment. It's a portrayal of God as faithful and compassionate. He's grieved, obviously—what good husband wouldn't be? And He clearly wants a change in His bride's wanton behavior. He wants marriage as it was designed to be: loving, intimate, fulfilling. The prophet's portrayal of God shows us the tender compassion of a heartbroken husband. In spite of all of Israel's "sleeping around" with other gods, God waits hopefully: "I will win her back once again. I will lead her into the desert and speak tenderly to her there. I will return her vineyards to her and transform the Valley of Trouble into a gateway of hope" (Hosea 2:14-15).

We don't live under the threat of Assyrian invasion, and our idolatry isn't likely to take the same shape as Israel's worship at pagan shrines. But we are in the same kind of relationship with the same God—an intimate union with the One who calls us to be His bride—so Hosea's portrait of God is extremely relevant. Though many Christians serve God out of obligation or wrestle with theology or follow a system of godly principles, behind the scenes is a God who longs for our affection and can be grieved when we give it to other loves. Our relationship with Him was never meant to be a religious exercise; it is meant to be a melding of hearts. This is why we were made, why God went to such great lengths to deal with our separation from Him, and what the Holy Spirit pursues in us daily. He wants our love.

We are never more aligned with our created purpose than when we give God our wholehearted love and let it define our lives. All attempts to master principles of faith, live holy lives, serve God, and affect the world for His Kingdom are futile without it. There's a reason Jesus said that the greatest commandment is to love God wholeheartedly. That is God's greatest desire for us. He is grieved without our love, and He waits patiently and faithfully for us to turn our affections to Him.

## QUESTIONS FOR REFLECTION

Why is unfaithfulness to God considered adultery? Why do you think the people of Israel kept turning their hearts to lesser gods? In what ways do we do that today?

 DAY 46

# JOEL

Joel prophesies about a plague of locusts. Or about an invading army. Or about both. No one is quite sure, and no one knows exactly when the prophecy was (or will be) fulfilled. What is clear, however, is that a "day of the LORD" is coming, which in prophetic books always seems to imply judgment. It is a day when God will no longer wait for people to respond; He will act based on how they have already responded. And that day is always spoken of in terms of awe and trembling.

Most likely, Joel, a prophet of the southern kingdom of Judah, uses a recent and devastating plague of locusts as a prophetic picture of another judgment to come, this time by an army that will devour the land more thoroughly than swarming locusts. Though God wants this nation to resemble His Kingdom—and His Garden from the beginning pages of Scripture—the coming warriors will rake over the land and remove any vestige of Eden. This coming judgment can be averted if the nation calls a solemn assembly and repents, sincerely and deeply, individually and corporately. After all, God has made a covenant to dwell among and within His people. He wants to restore them and to live in their midst. But there are conditions for hosting the presence of God in a nation or a group of people or even an individual life; the environment has to reflect His character and His purposes. If it doesn't, He must reshape it—usually a traumatic process—to be able to handle the weight of His glory.

God will restore the people and live in their midst eventually, of course, even if they don't have a change of heart now—which, as we know from history, they didn't. Somehow, God's calls to repentance are rarely recognized as being His voice until after the chastisement comes. Then it's clear that the voice was true. That's human nature; we don't want to heed a warning if the warning isn't legitimate, and in a world full of exaggerations and scare tactics, many warnings aren't. But some are, and it's up to us to discern the difference.

As with other prophets, Joel's words point both to immediate situations in Judah's current history and big-picture events in the ultimate future. They are simultaneously here-and-now and there-and-then. Peter picks up on Joel's prophecy that God will pour out His Spirit on all people. Sons and daughters will prophesy, old men will dream dreams, and young men will see visions. On men and women everywhere, the Spirit will flow. The sun will turn to darkness and the moon to blood through the smoke of God's wonders and judgment (Joel 2:28-32; Acts 2:17-21). Peter discerned the true flavor of these words, even though no one dreamed dreams or saw visions on the Day of Pentecost and the sun and moon stayed pretty much the same. There was no cataclysmic judgment, either literally or figuratively, on that day. But there was a rush of wind and flames like fire, and people spoke in other languages. A shift had taken place, and that shift was best described by Joel's prophetic imagery, which points to the Pentecostal outpouring as well as even greater phenomena to come. Peter's quote would hardly fit the criteria of theologians today in terms of using it with regard to context and original intent, but it certainly fits the Spirit's criteria of pointing to God's grand purposes. Apparently, prophetic glimpses can have far broader applications than we think they do.

That's how God's Word works. He speaks into an immediate situation, but His words echo throughout history, carrying with them the power to shape our lives and the future and to be fulfilled in something far greater than we originally envisioned. That's why the words of a prophet from more than two and a half millennia ago are never irrelevant to us. With the power of the eternal Holy Spirit behind them, they resonate in situations today as if they were spoken for our day and age.

## Questions for Reflection

What conditions does God place on His people in order for them to have a meaningful, vibrant relationship with Him? What role does repentance play in preparing for or preserving that relationship?

DAY 47

# AMOS

Amos is minding his own business—namely tending sheep and picking figs—when God gives him an uncomfortable assignment: go from the southern kingdom of Judah and prophesy a message of coming destruction to the king of the northern kingdom of Israel. Not surprisingly, that message is not well received by the king of Israel.

The message God gives Amos starts out as a rebuke to the nations surrounding Israel, including Assyria, Philistia, and Tyre (Lebanon today). At first, those who hear Amos are rather satisfied that the prophet supports their vision of the coming Day of the Lord, a day when God will exalt His people and bring down their enemies. But that's not how this "day of the Lord" will go down, as Amos sees it, because the judgment against nations includes Judah—very close brothers to Israel—and then Israel itself. Why? Because God's people are held to a higher standard, and this generation (as well as previous ones) has violated the covenant He established with them. So if Edom and Ammon and all the other nations who didn't receive God's instructions are judged for their acts of aggression, how much more will the chosen nation be punished for violating God's character, which was explicitly spelled out for them? It's an early expression of a later statement made by Jesus: "When someone has been given much, much will be required in return; and when someone has been entrusted with much, even more will be required" (Luke 12:48). The people of Israel have been given a lot, and yet they squandered their privilege. Next to God's plumb line, they are found to be crooked. God will chastise them harshly.

The words of Amos fall on deaf ears, in part because God offers very little evidence to back up His prophet. These are days of relative prosperity and stability in Israel, and the threat of Assyria—the strongest enemy around—has been waning. From all appearances, God is blessing His people, not getting ready to judge them. But Amos spells out their sins, most of which have to do with issues of justice. These days of prosperity have come at the expense of the poor among them; there is blatant exploitation among God's people. This alone should have pricked their consciences and made them reflect on their condition. But they have been comparing themselves with surrounding nations, not with the character of God, and this distorted perspective gives them plenty of room to tolerate their own flaws. As long as they are better than their neighbors, they reason, God must like them. Amos assures them that God has given them a higher calling than that.

This prophetic word illustrates a principle that we can easily apply to our own lives. We are far too ready to cater to our shortcomings when we see others around us who have much more obvious ones. "Well, at least I don't . . ." we tell ourselves. It's true that God has plenty of grace and that we can become unhealthily perfectionistic and unforgiving of ourselves. Yet it's also true that when God gives a special calling, He has high expectations. And every believer has been given a special calling—namely to conform to God's character—in addition to whatever assignment we've been given. God won't judge us for failing to live up to His character—otherwise we'd all live under constant judgment—but He certainly corrects us when we give up the pursuit. We may not be allowed to do what others can get away with. But even if we could, we still can never measure ourselves by others. That's a false standard, one that God has not given us. No, the standard is the one Amos calls Israel to follow: the nature of God Himself. If we aren't reflecting Him, we're reflecting something else. And that's a squandered opportunity to draw close to Him and positively affect others. We are always being called higher and deeper—regardless of the world around us.

## QUESTIONS FOR REFLECTION

How concerned do you think most Christians are about the issues in Amos—specifically oppression, injustice, exploitation of the poor, and similar social issues? Why? How does God want us to deal with such issues today?

 DAY 48

# OBADIAH

If the "minor prophets" are labeled as such for the brevity of their prophecies, then Obadiah deserves the title more than any. His "book" is a twenty-one-verse indictment against Edom that seldom makes its way into small group studies or pulpit sermons. That's because it doesn't have sound-bite packaging, a feel-good purpose, or a broad application—at least on the surface. After all, how often do pesky Edomites pillage our cities today? But Obadiah does have powerful messages in it for those who will look. In fact, when we read between the lines of this short book, it is profoundly encouraging.

This Obadiah is not the same one from Elijah's time, the one who hid prophets in caves when Jezebel attempted to purge Israel of Yahweh worship. Historically, this prophet fits much better after Jerusalem's fall, because he speaks of the time when the Babylonians carried off the city's wealth and cast lots for its land. The Edomites—descendants of Jacob's brother Esau—did not behave like family on that day. Instead, they stood apart from the city's downfall. Some even participated in it or looted the city as it lay in ruins. Instead of siding with their distant cousins in Judah, they joined hands with the foreign invaders and celebrated the destruction of the Temple. They betrayed their neighbors and their own heritage.

Obadiah condemns this, of course, and foretells Edom's destruction. Though from all outward appearances Judah is destroyed and Edom thrives, the reverse is actually true. Judah will be restored and Edom will be wiped off the map. That's God's assessment of the situation, and it's truer than outward appearances. Edom's celebration will not last.

What does this prophecy tell us about life? That we reap what we sow—a sobering message if what we've sown is destruction and devastation, but an encouraging one if we've sown things such as comfort, peace, and generosity. Clearly this message isn't confined to Obadiah; it's a solid theme scattered throughout Scripture. It makes sense of the Cross—we've sown seeds of rebellion, and Jesus reaped the consequences on our behalf—but in general, even after the Cross, the Bible affirms this law of nature: Whatever we dish out, we must be ready to receive in return. That can be alarming, but Jesus pointed out the opportunity in this principle. When we give away our love and forgiveness and all other goodness, we can expect it to be given back to us. Whatever measure we use for others will be used for us in return (Luke 6:38). Because the Edomites were brutally merciless, Obadiah says that's the harvest they can expect. But we can go to the other extreme and reap a harvest of goodness beyond our dreams.

What does Obadiah's message tell us about God? That He defends His people, even when they are on the uncomfortable end of His judgments. Yes, He has disciplined Judah and allowed Jerusalem to be destroyed, but that's family business. On a playground full of bullies, He's the ultimate big brother. He will rise up to defend a family member, even if He had an issue with that same family member at the breakfast table just this morning. He can discipline us at will, but anyone else who tries to mess with us will have to deal with the consequences of His wrath. He guards His own.

Most of all, we can learn from this little book that God wants us to reflect His heart. The Edomites gloated over their enemy's downfall—an attitude condemned in Proverbs 24:17—and celebrated at exactly the wrong time. They rejoiced while God grieved. Being out of sync with God's heartbeat is a sure way to miss out on His plan. But the reverse can be true as well: When we are sensitive to what God is doing, we are brought into His plan and even given significant roles in it. We, like Judah, find that He strongly supports those whose hearts will synchronize with His.

## QUESTIONS FOR REFLECTION

How does the principle that we reap what we sow apply to us in light of our salvation? How can we use that principle to our benefit?

 DAY 49

# JONAH

On the surface, the book of Jonah seems to be the story of a reluctant prophet who needs to learn a hard lesson in obedience. But it really goes much deeper than that. Interestingly, the book comes immediately after Obadiah, which rebukes the unmerciful Edomites, whose hearts did not align with God's. Now we are given an example of a prophet who has the same problem, albeit centuries earlier. This time, the situation is also reversed. This patriotic prophet would love nothing more than to see Israel's dreaded enemy, the Assyrian city of Nineveh, suffer under God's judgment. But God has another plan.

The story begins when God tells Jonah to go to Nineveh and

preach against its sins—a task not unlike going to Red Square in the 1960s and loudly proclaiming the evils of communism or traveling to Mecca today to declare the errors of Islam in a public square. It seems like a pointless suicide mission, as Assyria is known for its brutal treatment of enemies and Israel certainly fits that category. Yet God has spoken. So what does the prophet do? He tries to get as far away from God as possible. The open seas, a long way from the Promised Land, should do the trick. Jonah buys a ticket westward.

But God is very present at sea and even sovereign over its creatures. A storm threatens the ship, and Jonah's guilty conscience tells him why. He confesses his rebellion against God and volunteers to be the sacrificial scapegoat, telling his shipmates to throw him into the sea—perhaps another attempt to escape God's call, this time through death. But God gives the prophet some time to think in the belly of a fish, and after Jonah repents, the fish coughs him up on land. He is given a second chance.

Though prophets such as Jeremiah and Isaiah later preach thousands of words without seeing any results, Jonah delivers a very uninspiring, one-sentence sermon and sees an entire pagan city, one steeped in violence and idolatry, turn to God.

At this point we find out the real reason Jonah fled; he may have feared for his life, but he was even more afraid that God would show mercy to Nineveh. He protests God's compassion toward the evil city and asks to die. God uses a vine to give Jonah an object lesson—pointing out the senseless position of a prophet who has compassion for a withered plant and his own comfort, but not for a people who do not know their Creator. God has compassion for those who are lost and broken, and Jonah misses His heart completely. The last verse of the book sums it up: "Shouldn't I feel sorry for such a great city?" (Jonah 4:11). The implication is that God is concerned, so His prophet should be as well.

That's the dominant theme of this prophetic picture: God loves even the worst of rebels. That love didn't show through in His judgment of Edom in Obadiah's prophecy, but Edom had a much longer track record of rejecting God's overtures. The Assyrians are offered a chance to turn to God, and they take it. Apparently it doesn't last—the nation will later harden its heart and invade Israel, and they will be judged for it—but in Jonah's generation, God's mercy changes Ninevite hearts. This is a God with a global agenda.

Again we see God inviting His people to share His heartbeat. He doesn't want His people merely to know about His thoughts and feelings. He wants them to bond with Him there. This portrayal of God at the end of the book of Jonah is a perfect illustration of what God intended by making us in His own image. The portrayal of Jonah is a stark illustration of what was lost when our connection with God was damaged in the Fall. The biblical narrative is an epic tale of restoration. When God invites us to share His heart—about anything, even our dreaded enemies—we recapture a little more of that connection.

## QUESTIONS FOR REFLECTION

Why did God want Jonah to share His heart for the Ninevites? Why was that difficult for Jonah? In what ways does God want us to share His heart today? In what ways is that difficult for you? Why?

 DAY 50

# MICAH

In Romans 12:9, Paul urges God's people to hate what is evil and cling to what is good. Apparently, in Micah's day, the people did just the opposite (Micah 3:2). This prophecy proclaims judgment against Judah for its sin—specifically its acts of injustice, corruption, and exploitation of society's most vulnerable citizens. The upper class is seizing property and defrauding people of their inheritances—gross evils in the eyes of God. Like Amos and other prophets, Micah expresses God's heart for social justice.

Micah prophesies about the same time as Isaiah—probably after Israel was conquered by Assyria but well before Judah is taken captive by Babylon. Like Isaiah, Micah sees ungodly practices among the people who have been called to represent God's character in the world, and he calls them out for it. The nation's leaders are corrupt. Businessmen lack integrity and honest scales. Neighbors aren't trustworthy. Not only have the rich and powerful exploited the poor and weak, but many of the nation's prophets have covered up the spiritual implications of their exploitation. They have declared peace where there is no peace, implying that God has no complaint against His people. "All is well," they say. But all is not well. God cannot and will not allow these injustices to continue. So, contrary to the prevailing mood of the day, Micah and a few other true prophets of the time proclaim the sober truth. And the declarations of judgment are severe.

Yet like Isaiah, Micah also catches glimpses of a messianic golden age. Some of his descriptions in prophetic figurative language seem to fit the ministry of Jesus; some seem to point to His Second Coming, when the messianic age will be established in full. One key prophecy fueled messianic watchmen for the next several centuries: Out of Bethlehem will come a ruler of Israel. After all the judgment comes a Savior.

One of the most intriguing scenes in Micah is the lawsuit God brings against His people. In chapter 6, the Lord invites His people to plead their case before Him with the mountains and hills as witnesses. The law boils down to a few requirements: "The LORD has told you what is good, and this is what he requires of you: to do what is right, to love mercy, and to walk humbly with your God" (Micah 6:8). It's simple, but the people have even failed at this. They haven't done justice or loved mercy or even walked humbly with their Creator. So the verdict in this cosmic courtroom is *guilty*. The punishment has already been planned (Micah 6:13), and it's a harsh sentence.

When the church today speaks of sin, we often immediately think of sexual immorality, drunkenness, and other licentious behaviors. But prophets such as Micah are far more preoccupied with a lack of integrity and compassion toward the downtrodden and justice for all who are oppressed—sins that many Christians are almost casual about today. The prophets are vigorous in insisting that God's people must reflect His character. Where He is merciful, we should be merciful. Where He does justice, we should do justice. We can't have a lying tongue or use false measurements because God doesn't have a lying tongue or resort to false measurements. The "I'm only human" excuse doesn't fly in the courtroom of a God of integrity. He doesn't just want people who obey; He wants people who *want* to be like Him. He wants hearts conformed to His in every area of life.

To our relief, the guilty verdict isn't the final status for God's people, as Micah echoes the restoration other prophets have foretold. As Jeremiah and Ezekiel will later prophesy, God will take care of the heart issues of His people. He will give them new hearts—ones that are ethical and compassionate and cut from the same cloth as His. This is the divine privilege of those who become God's children, and it results in a Kingdom that looks as if it is ruled by a Messiah who tramples our sins under His feet and throws them into the depths of the ocean (Micah 7:19). The heart of the King and the hearts of His people become one. And the Kingdom is filled with justice, mercy, and those who walk humbly with their God.

## QUESTIONS FOR REFLECTION

What are the spiritual dangers of living in a complacent, prosperous society? Why do you think many Christians tend to see sexual immorality as more sinful than ethical immorality?

 DAY 51

# NAHUM

We see a few glimpses of Assyria's spiritual history in Scripture, and they show us how a patient God deals with a hard and militaristic people. God has given them opportunities to turn to Him, and for a brief time some did—that's what the book of Jonah is about. But after a waning of influence and then another crescendo to power for Assyria, God uses the empire to overthrow the northern kingdom of Israel in 722 BC. The southern kingdom of Judah becomes something of a vassal state—semi-independent but paying tribute to Assyria and having to endure threats of invasion. By the time Nahum writes, roughly a century after Israel's downfall, Assyria is equated with pride and brutal violence. And God's patience has run its course.

So Nahum prophesies judgment against Nineveh, the capital of Assyrian power, and the judgment is irrevocable. When Jonah prophesied a terse message against the same city—"Forty days from now Nineveh will be destroyed!" (Jonah 3:4)—there was apparently still an opportunity to receive God's mercy, because the city turned to Him and was spared. But Nahum's prophecy is final. It's too late. "Your injury is fatal," says the prophet to the foreign king (Nahum 3:19). The lying and violence of "the city of blood" (Nahum 3:1, NIV) will come back upon its people. God protects those who trust in Him, but He will sweep away the enemies of His people. And at this point, there's nothing the Ninevites can do about it.

We see a similar judgment against a foreign nation in Obadiah, but the target of Nahum's prophecy is much bigger and more threatening. This prophecy is a clear statement that the long-suffering God does not put up with rebellion forever. He allows empires, even evil ones, to rise to power, but they will not last. Littered across the landscape of history are numerous examples: From Babylon to Nazi Germany and beyond, those who oppress God's people eventually become distant memories on the wrong side of God's story. This is terrible news for those who have chosen aggression and violence in their quest for power, but it's immensely reassuring for those who endure oppression under evil rulers.

The message of Nahum is bigger than reassurances about empires and injustice. On a much larger scale, it's a picture of how God will judge evil as a whole. We live in a world that is at times excruciating. God's creation is beautiful, but it's broken, reeling under the weight of human rebellion. We experience pain and heartache, sometimes more than we think we can handle. But even though evil runs rampant throughout the world, God has it on a leash. He is sovereign over it. He keeps it within limits. Evil has an expiration date, and its clock is winding down.

Depending on where one stands spiritually, the opening words of Nahum's prophecy are either comforting or terrifying: "The LORD is a jealous God, filled with vengeance and rage. He takes revenge on all who oppose him and continues to rage against his enemies!" (Nahum 1:2). Like a passionate lover, God zealously stands up for His beloved. The final judgment of Nineveh is a graphic foreshadowing of the final judgment in Revelation. Regardless of how life looks right now, God is relentlessly determined to establish those He loves and remove anyone who hurts them. He *will* fulfill His promises. Nothing can thwart His goodness toward those who belong to Him. He is always on our side.

## QUESTIONS FOR REFLECTION

How do you feel when you read headlines that show the world as unstable and threatening? How easy or difficult is it for you to rest in God's sovereignty over global events?

 DAY 52

# HABAKKUK

The psalmist Asaph looked around him and saw evil people prospering while faithful people suffered (Psalm 73). That picture didn't look like anything God had promised, or even anything that fit the plans of a God of justice, and Asaph wondered why. Only when he got into God's presence did he see the bigger picture and choose to trust his Creator.

Habakkuk's prophecy follows a similar trajectory. He is full of questions right from the start. How long does he have to cry out before God answers? Why does God tolerate injustice? Why does the nation suffer from the sins of its own people? On and on he goes, pouring out complaints that most might think but few would express. But God answers Habakkuk, at least in part. He tells the prophet He is about to do something amazing. He will raise up the Babylonians—a ruthless, proud, violent people who have made a god out of their own strength—to become His instrument of judgment. Then that nation will be judged for its ruthlessness, pride, and violence.

This is a common theme in the time leading up to Judah's

captivity, but Habakkuk's style and methods are anything but common. This prophecy never addresses human beings directly; it's an ongoing conversation between the prophet and God. The blunt honesty with which Habakkuk addresses God is reminiscent of Job, Jeremiah, and even Jacob's wrestling match with the divine presence. And though that sort of honesty is often looked down upon by the most reverent of God's people, it seems perfectly welcomed here. Not only does God answer, but He also promises deeper revelation and unveils at least part of His plan for the prophet to see. The result is that Habakkuk, much like Asaph, is transformed by the end of his own writing. He moves from complaints to patience and trust as God accomplishes His purposes.

God accepts a brutally honest relationship with His people because, after all, we were created for relationship with Him. And what's a relationship without honesty? If there's something wrong with our attitude, some perception that needs to be reshaped, God will reshape it—just as He did with Habakkuk. He seems to much prefer those who will wrestle with Him to those who bury the things they want to wrestle over. This is where relationships are established, forged, and deepened. God enjoys the interaction—even when we're unsettled in the process.

Habakkuk gives us a profound glimpse into how we can hear from God. He stands watch, and he waits to "see" what God will say—further confirmation that God often speaks in pictures. He is told to write down the revelation and then wait for it, even if the fulfillment seems to tarry. He is to be patient with God's timing.

That waiting process seems to be where the book ends, and Habakkuk is fine with that. He is not filled with complaints like he was at the beginning. Even when there seems to be zero evidence of God's goodness—though the fig trees, grape vines, and olive trees are barren, and though there's no more livestock in the stalls—he will rejoice in God. In other words, he has settled the question of God's goodness in his heart. The lifelong struggle we face to believe in the good heart of God during trying times is no longer a battle for Habakkuk. He is determined to have joy regardless of the circumstances.

In many ways, this is the essence of the faith of the righteous—declared in Habakkuk 2:4 and quoted often in the New Testament as the manner in which we receive salvation. The righteous shall live by faith that God will accomplish His purposes, that His words are true, that He is relentlessly good—and that even when we don't understand our circumstances, He is working. Not only are we able to endure in those circumstances, we can thrive in them. When we see who God is and choose to believe, He will give us feet like a deer's so we can ascend to the highest mountains with Him.

## QUESTIONS FOR REFLECTION

How do you think Habakkuk was able to settle the question of God's goodness in his heart? What was the key to finding joy in spite of circumstances?

DAY 53

# ZEPHANIAH

Zephaniah was a descendant of a godly king (Hezekiah), and he prophesies during the reign of another godly king (Josiah). So why are his prophecies so severe? Why does he foretell catastrophe for Judah in such grim language? Why do his warnings repeatedly refer to "the LORD of hosts," the God of heaven's warriors? Because in spite of Judah's occasional reformist kings, the country is still influenced by idolatry. No matter how much Josiah tries to tear down the altars of Baal and Molech, unholy altars remain. Why? Because idolatry is a matter of the heart. Kings and priests can remove the outward evidence, but if a heart is inclined to worship a pagan god, altars will spring up again.

That's what happens in Judah in the latter days of its nationhood. There are efforts to revitalize Temple worship of God, but many throughout the country still retain their household shrines or hillside altars to false gods. They aren't particularly defiant about it, for the most part; they simply believe God doesn't care or is too distant or detached to be bothered by their private worship practices. They are casual about their spirituality, not realizing that God is anything but casual about the worship of His people. So Zephaniah pronounces a coming judgment, a refrain Jeremiah will soon pick up with even more detail and dread. God's anger will be poured out, and it will be "a day of terrible distress and anguish, a day of ruin and desolation, a day of darkness and gloom, a day of clouds and blackness" (Zephaniah 1:15). The judgment is depicted in violent terms befitting the Babylonian conquest, which will fulfill the prophet's words some three or four decades later. At times, the meaning of the words seems even larger than that, as if it points to a greater judgment at a much later time in human history. But for the generation to whom Zephaniah preaches, these words are alarmingly immediate. In less than one generation, Judah and Jerusalem will be judged.

Why does a God of love speak so harshly to His beloved people? Because love isn't complacent. It can't be—not when the beloved are destroying themselves and defiling the purpose for which they were created. Not when gentle rebukes have done nothing to jar them from their complacency. Not when the stakes are as high as life and death at the deepest spiritual level. In fact, love can't respond any other way. If a victim of heart failure is at the brink of death, those emergency paddles that violently shock the body can be lifesaving. If spiritually complacent people are sabotaging their own destiny, shockingly strong words may be the only remedy that works.

Perhaps that's why the compassionate, loving Jesus pronounced harsh words of woe on the religious leaders of His time. Complacency and stubborn hearts are enemies of life, and Jesus came to bring life in its fullest sense, not just to Israel but to the world. Zephaniah points to Christ's mission, in fact, when he foretells entire nations coming to God (Zephaniah 3:9). This global outlook is rare among Hebrew prophets; usually they predict restoration for Israel and Judah (after judgment), but only judgment for their neighbors. But apart from Isaiah before him and Zechariah after him, Zephaniah is one of the few to envision a salvation beyond the borders of Israel. God's people will become the centerpiece of His saving work.

That's how the prophecy ends. In spite of all its violent words of judgment, it leaves us with a profound picture of a God who delights in His people (now restored and with purified hearts) and even rejoices over them with singing. He holds them in His arms like a baby and deals with them tenderly. Yes, He has been harsh, but He is also mighty to save. He will bring them back. Regardless of what they have been through, His love calms all their fears and His heart beats with the joy of a thoroughly devoted parent.

## QUESTIONS FOR REFLECTION

To what degree do you think today's church is spiritually complacent? Why is complacency such a dangerous condition? How does it affect you to know that God holds His people in His arms and sings over them?

DAY 54

# HAGGAI

Most people believe that the primary purpose of prophecy is to predict the future. After reading the Hebrew prophets, one might also get the impression that prophecy is all about bad news—a future worth dreading. But prophecy is simply speaking God's words and expressing His heart in a situation. Sometimes that means predicting the future, and sometimes it means issuing strong warnings, but it doesn't have to involve either. In the New Testament, Paul says it's for strengthening, encouraging, and comforting others (1 Corinthians 14:3). The purpose is to express God's voice. And God's voice can be filled with motivating, inspiring words.

Haggai is a good example of Paul's description of prophecy. Here the prophet strengthens, encourages, and comforts his readers. He prophesies after the exiles have returned to Jerusalem under the leadership of Zerubbabel, a governor and descendant of David, and Joshua, a descendant of the last high priest. The reconstruction of the Temple began almost immediately upon their return, but it has stalled due to fierce opposition from local residents and apathy among God's people. Haggai urges the people to work hard to finish the project, promising that the renewed covenant means renewed promises and a renewed presence of the Lord. God will bless all other nations through this nation—that hasn't changed—but only if they give Him His proper place in their hearts and lives. The Messiah will come through the house of David to bring His Kingdom to the world, as promised. This is a profound destiny, not an occasion for apathy.

Haggai's purpose is to motivate, to stir up the apathetic and provoke them to diligence. They are to focus on God's work above their own interests. Their pursuit of God's presence should be far more important to them than their pursuit of economic well-being—a message perhaps needed even more in our times than in Haggai's.

This issue of the Temple shows us again that God deeply desires to dwell among His people. That isn't to say He hasn't been with them in Babylon and Persia, or long before in Egypt, or wherever they are on earth. But He longs for a place of meeting—first a Tabernacle, then a Temple, then human flesh, and then a temple made up of millions of human hearts. In Haggai's time, the building is more than a building; it's a litmus test. God desires to manifest Himself among the people. Do they desire the same? It's a question extremely relevant to our own lives, for we know God has made His intentions clear about residing with us and in us. Do we prioritize His presence? If not, we are in the same condition as Haggai's readers.

This condition has adverse consequences, if not corrected. Haggai is forthright in claiming that the people missed out on God's blessings when they weren't committed to Him. They suffered economic hardship because they focused solely on their own welfare. There's no rain, and the harvests are bad. Why? Because God's house remains a ruin (Haggai 1:9). We may be reluctant to attribute cause and effect to our faithfulness—bad things do happen to faithful people, after all, and good things happen to faithless people. But in this case, neglecting the place of God's presence clearly results in poverty. It's a dynamic that's still true today. The place of God's presence has changed—there is no Temple building, for God now dwells within us—but the truth remains. When we fail to cultivate a sense of His presence, we shouldn't be surprised if we experience hardship.

When we are diligent about God's presence, His favor manifests itself in various ways in our lives. Like Israel, we find that restoration is not just a consolation prize for a failed life. When God restores us, our failures and subsequent redemption actually catapult us further than we were before. The glory of God's latter house is always greater than the glory of the former (Haggai 2:9). Just as redeemed humanity has a deeper connection with God and a greater glory than Adam and Eve before the Fall, so God's response to our worst failures can elevate us to higher places than we were before we failed. The promise of Romans 8:28—that God works all things together for good for those who love Him—is more than consolation. It is a means to God's greatest blessings.

## QUESTIONS FOR REFLECTION

What are some actions or attitudes in our lives that demonstrate our level of hunger for God's presence? What can we do to position ourselves to experience more of His presence? How do you think God responds when we clearly prioritize Him in every area of life?

 DAY 55

# ZECHARIAH

Not long after Haggai encouraged the returned exiles to continue rebuilding the Temple, Zechariah had a series of visions that reinforced that theme. The first six chapters of his prophecy are dreamlike scenes—a red horse, a flying scroll, a woman of wickedness in a basket, and other provocative images—strange glimpses behind the veil that divides the natural world from the supernatural realm. These visions seem disconnected at times, as dream sequences often do, but they all point to worship, the Temple project, and God's restoration of His people. One of the most encouraging (and least obscure) visions is of Joshua the high priest, who stands before God while the adversary relentlessly accuses him for Israel's offenses. The Lord Himself rebukes Satan, defends Joshua, clothes the priest in robes of righteousness, and gives him sacred assignments—a powerful picture of restored purity that soothes guilty consciences even today. Joshua is clean simply because God has declared him so. The adversary has nothing to say in response.

This behind-the-scenes look at the spiritual realm fits in the category we call "apocalyptic literature," in the sense that they unveil what is hidden. The book of Revelation quotes extensively from Zechariah (and Daniel and Ezekiel) and echoes many of its themes. These heavenly glimpses encourage those who are pressed under the weight of visible circumstances—in some cases persecution and in the case of Zechariah's audience, obstacles and overwhelming odds. In their vulnerable state, the people need to know that God Himself will be a wall of fire around Jerusalem and its glory within (Zechariah 2:5). This is the reality they need to see.

The last six chapters of Zechariah are thoroughly messianic. The New Testament writers quote these passages extensively, finding in them a savior-king who comes riding on a donkey, a shepherd bought for thirty pieces of silver, a shepherd being struck and his sheep scattered, and God's people looking on the one they have pierced. These prophecies look forward to the very end when the Lord Himself stands on the Mount of Olives while an earthquake rearranges the landscape and fills the land with living water flowing from Jerusalem. More than any Old Testament book other than Isaiah, Zechariah gives us pictures of the Messiah's present and future work.

The intensity of God's love for His people also appears more in Zechariah than in most other books. These are the prophecies that call His beloved the apple of His eye (Zechariah 2:8, NASB), and in surprisingly emotional terms, declare that He burns with jealousy over His people (Zechariah 8:2, NASB). Burning jealousy makes quite a few people uncomfortable when applied to the divine—isn't God more stable and secure than that?—but we've already seen His relentless love throughout the pages of Scripture. When true love is thwarted because the beloved throws herself at lesser lovers, jealousy is the only appropriate response. God deeply desires wholehearted devotion from His beloved. The prophecies of Zechariah mean to make sure He gets it.

So the obstacles for wholehearted devotion are removed. Are God's people depending on their own abilities in life? It doesn't matter—it's not by might or strength but by God's power (Zechariah 4:6). Are they measuring their progress negatively? No one should despise the day of small things (Zechariah 4:10, NASB). Are they depending on their own righteousness? Righteousness is a matter of God's choosing, not human effort (Zechariah 3:1-2). There is no requirement that God has not fully equipped His people to fulfill through His power and purity. All they have to do is return to the Lord, and He will return to them (Zechariah 1:3). When our hearts finally lean fully toward God, His zeal fills the gap between us with everything we need.

## Questions for Reflection

How does it make you feel to know that God burns with jealousy over the inclination of your heart? What needs to happen in our hearts for God's desire for us to be satisfied?

 DAY 56

# MALACHI

Haggai and Zechariah foretold a greater glory coming to God's people and to His Temple—a messianic age in which God's presence would be manifest and the influence of His people would be global. About eighty years later, the people have reason to be disappointed in those unfulfilled prophecies. God has not filled His Temple in any tangible sense, miracles aren't happening, and Judah remains a small, out-of-the-way territory under a much larger empire. Where is the God of glory?

He is coming, says Malachi. The prophet, whose name means "my messenger," is a contemporary of Ezra and Nehemiah and plays a part in turning complacent hearts back to the Lord. He emphasizes the covenant: God has been faithful, but His people have been unfaithful in their worship, in their behavior toward each other, and in their marriages. God has chosen Jacob—the house of Israel—over all others. Yet they are questioning God's commitment, His presence, and even His sense of justice. They see the wicked prospering and assume God doesn't care anymore. So, in a sense, they behave as if they don't care anymore. The priests are casual about their offerings, which in many cases have been grudgingly brought to them by people who are making offerings to God simply out of a sense of duty. Even many of the fine, upstanding leaders of the community are breaking faith in their marriages. God hates divorce, Malachi tells them—even while Ezra and Nehemiah are compelling them to divorce their idolatrous wives and send them away. They have assumed a lifestyle and an attitude common to many in this world: outwardly religious and inwardly ambivalent toward God.

This, according to Malachi, is why their offerings don't seem to be accepted. But to everyone who has asked where God is—to those who lament that there is no glory in the second Temple, nor are there crops in the fields—Malachi declares that the Lord Himself is coming to His Temple. And a messenger of the covenant is coming too. But God is coming as a refining fire, not as a satisfier of religious curiosities. He will purify His people.

This is encouraging news for those who love God wholeheartedly and painful news for those whose worship and faithfulness are halfhearted. Malachi urges a turning, an embracing of the refining process even now. If the people would only be generous toward God—that is, if they would cease "robbing" Him (Malachi 3:8-9)—they would find Him to be overwhelmingly generous toward them. If they will learn what the word *covenant* implies—in their relationships with Him and with each other—they will experience the covenant's blessings. If they will treat each other fairly, they will be able to see God as a God of justice, even when His justice seems slow in coming. If they live according to God's character, they will realize God's character.

God's character is a recurring scriptural theme. In a sense, He allows us to choose the climate of our relationship with Him. If we don't embrace things such as mercy, faithfulness, and generosity, we're not very likely to experience His mercy, faithfulness, and generosity in practical ways. God's character doesn't change, of course, but the blessings of His Kingdom often hinge on whether we accept the culture of His Kingdom. When we gratefully embrace His goodness, He shows us more of it.

Malachi is the last writing prophet to be included in the Old Testament, so it's fitting that his name points to the messenger who will prepare the way for the Messiah. An Elijah will come and turn the hearts of fathers back to their children (Malachi 4:5-6), just as a Son will come and reconcile the Father with a fallen race of people who have little knowledge of His heart. And the curse that has caused such brokenness throughout history, even among God's own people, will be undone.

## QUESTIONS FOR REFLECTION

In what ways, if any, have you been disappointed with God's work in your life? What do you think God would say about your disappointments? In what ways, and to what degree, do our responses to God determine our experience of Him?

DAY 57

# THE NEW TESTAMENT

More than four hundred years have passed since Malachi prophesied, prompting many people to call these "the silent years" before the coming of the New Testament. But it's hard to imagine the living Word being silent; He must have spoken to quite a few people during these centuries, even though He didn't inspire anyone to write additional Scripture.[1] In fact, quite a bit happened during these centuries as God prepared His people for the coming of the Messiah. Needs and frustrations intensified. Expectations were raised. In the fullness of time, the Messiah would come and be recognized by those with ears to hear and eyes to see.

But the waiting period for Judah isn't easy. The predictions of its later prophets have not yet materialized. God's people are still under foreign domination, though the foreign powers have kept changing—Persia, Greece, Rome, and various sub-powers within those vast empires, such as the Ptolemaic and Seleucid rulers. The people have experienced some victories, most notably the one celebrated at Hanukkah, which commemorates the Maccabean revolt that recovered the Temple from a Seleucid tyrant who had defiled it. But mostly they wait. We will see their longing embodied in two people in the Gospel of Luke—Anna the prophetess and Simeon the righteous, who are sensitive enough to the Holy Spirit to recognize the infant Jesus as Savior when His parents bring Him to the Temple to dedicate Him. And we see that longing in the many questions and speculations about the adult Jesus—whether He is "the prophet" foretold by Moses, the "Elijah" prophesied by Malachi, or the long-awaited Messiah Himself. As the Gospels open, many people are looking for that rescuer, and some are even

---

1 Orthodox and Roman Catholic canons do consider some writings from this era to be scriptural.

claiming to be Him. But only one figure makes a dramatic mark on history.

In this time between the Testaments, we get the sense that the pain of brokenness is deepening and the longing for a rescuer is increasing. The world is pregnant with the hope of God's intervention, even feeling the discomfort of being long overdue. In fact, that's the image a later writer will use when he explains that Jesus came in the fullness of time (Galatians 4:4). As civilizations rise and fall and the fulfillment of prophecies linger, people cry out for a savior.

That's not just the story of people in the centuries leading up to Jesus; it's our story too. We all long for a Savior. We want life to be fulfilling, for things to work out, to be rescued from the pain and brokenness of our own lives. Yes, some people accept the status quo and become independent spirits navigating the world on their own, but deep down they know a godless existence leads nowhere. It's futile. We are designed to live forever, created with yearnings for the eternal, and we can't be satisfied with a world in which civilizations rise and fall and nothing ultimately matters. If our experience has taught us anything, it's that we crave meaning and purpose. And if the Hebrew Scriptures have taught us anything, it's that we can have meaning and purpose. We can legitimately look forward to times of resolution and fulfillment, times when everything is fixed and there's no more pain or tears. Our hearts and our faith point us toward hope, and so does God's Word. The desire of all nations is coming. As a wise man told us, "Hope deferred makes the heart sick, but a longing fulfilled is a tree of life" (Proverbs 13:12, NIV). In the writings that follow, those longings begin to be fulfilled.

## QUESTIONS FOR REFLECTION

In what ways do you crave meaning and purpose in life? How have you longed for God to show Himself in your life and make things right? Why do you think God sometimes waits so long to fulfill His promises?

DAY 58

# MATTHEW 1–16

Like all of the Gospel writers—and really all communicators everywhere—Matthew has an agenda. He wants Jews to see Jesus as the Messiah of Hebrew prophecy, the heir to David's kingdom, and the fulfillment of God's promise to Abraham. He also wants Gentiles to see Jesus as the Savior, not just of the Jews, but of the world. Granted, this is a pretty broad agenda, but this Gospel is written to a pretty broad audience. Both Jews and Gentiles who have heard about the Messiah are still trying to understand who He is.

So the writer of this Gospel—traditionally Matthew, also known as the disciple Levi—alternates between narrating events and recording Jesus' discourses in order to present a picture of this king sent from God. After presenting a genealogy that establishes Jesus as a descendant of David, Matthew begins with a birth narrative—he and Luke are the only ones to do so—in which Herod the Great feels threatened by this new rival and attempts to eliminate Him. In events reminiscent of the life of Moses, the raging ruler murders innocent children while God helps Mary and Joseph navigate the treacherous circumstances through warnings in dreams.

As an adult, Jesus is revealed to be the Son of God at His baptism, and immediately another kind of enemy tries to tempt Him and question His identity. But He overcomes these obstacles and begins His world-transforming ministry with teachings such as those found in the Sermon on the Mount. This Kingdom is altogether different from what Herod expected—and from what the Jewish people expected, for that matter. In Matthew, Jesus' teachings describe the culture of this Kingdom, and His miracles depict its power. His first words tell us that the Kingdom is near, and the rest of the Gospel shows us just how near it is.

Again and again, Matthew quotes Jesus' sayings about what the Kingdom is like. It's like a mustard seed, like yeast, like a treasure hidden in a field or a dragnet cast into the sea. Jesus describes attitudes that are blessed by God because they accurately represent the character of the Kingdom. And He sends out His disciples with a Kingdom agenda: "Go and announce to them that the Kingdom of Heaven is near. Heal the sick, raise the dead, cure those with leprosy, and cast out demons. Give as freely as you have received!" (Matthew 10:7-8).

Clearly, Jesus is from God. But is He "the One"? Sitting in prison, John the Baptist isn't sure Jesus is the Messiah who sets captives free. Even after seeing Jesus' miracles, the citizens of Bethsaida and Korazin haven't turned to Him. Meanwhile, opposition mounts. The religious leadership, for the most part, is convinced that this Sabbath-breaker who tells pointed parables is a problem and a threat. Questions persist about who this Messiah is and what kind of kingdom He represents.

This tension builds throughout the Gospel of Matthew, culminating in a scene in the far northern reaches of Israel. Jesus asks His disciples who people say He is, and Peter nails the answer: the Messiah, the Son of the living God. Jesus firmly warns the disciples not to tell anyone yet, and then He sets His face resolutely toward Jerusalem with an ominous mission that no one understands. He's going there to die.

Yes, this is a different kind of king. Israel's expectations for a governing ruler aren't wrong, but they are mistimed. Jesus will fulfill that role at a later date, when He returns in victory. For now, He is a king who conquers through ultimate humiliation and the most unexpected means. And the question He poses to His disciples in Matthew 16:15—"Who do you say I am?"—lingers not only throughout the rest of this Gospel and the New Testament, but down to the present day as well. It echoes in our lives almost constantly. Who is Jesus in the midst of the problems we face today? Who is He in the relationships we're dealing with? Who is He in the dreams and desires that fill our hearts? Even when we've answered that question in one moment of decision, we still must apply the answer in practical terms every day. The Kingdom of God must become a reality in every area of our lives.

## QUESTIONS FOR REFLECTION

What aspects of God's Kingdom do you long for most? How is Jesus working His Kingdom into your life? How is He working it into the world around you?

 DAY 59

# MATTHEW 17–28

Soon after the great confession that He is the Messiah, Jesus takes three of His disciples up a high mountain and is "transfigured." They see Him—along with Moses and Elijah—in an altered, eternal state of glory, His brightness both dazzling and terrifying. Again He tells His followers not to say anything about what they have seen; He is guarding His identity carefully. In fact, we later see what happens when the crowds recognize Him as the anointed king. He comes riding into Jerusalem on a donkey—a gesture full of Davidic and messianic implications—and within a week the crowds have become disillusioned when He refuses to live up to their political expectations. He knows the time between the crowd's praise of Him and His death will be short. The people are just that fickle.

In the meantime, the disciples have to settle for knowing who He is without sharing it—and without understanding His enigmatic predictions of death. They will hear Him utter awkward and uncomfortable judgments against the religious elite, suggestions that God will cast out all hypocrites and put the Kingdom in the hands of those whose hearts are right. Jesus uses language that redefines what it means to be Israel, implying that many non-Jews will be fully included as God's chosen people. Though Jesus said that He came for the lost sheep of Israel, by the end of the Gospel the scope of His mission includes everyone. His disciples will be sent out to make disciples of all nations. All nations will appear before Him to be judged. Though God never revokes His promises to Israel, the Messiah's mission is much less centered on Israel—and much more merciful to outsiders—than the Hebrew sages of the time believed.

Meanwhile, Jesus has extremely ominous words for Israel's leaders and, more broadly, for the nation itself. He predicts the devastation of Jerusalem and the destruction of the Temple within the next generation. His words of judgment have cosmic overtones and are still hotly debated today. Does "the end of the age" spoken of in Matthew 24 apply to Israel or to all of history—or both? Does calamity come upon the land or the earth—or both? Is the picture of judgment for Jerusalem or for humanity as a whole—or both? Many of Jesus' words are clearly about Israel; others clearly go beyond. Regardless, they cause quite a stir.

What follows is a detailed account of Jesus' betrayal, trial, crucifixion, and resurrection. All the Gospel writers spend at least a quarter of their accounts on this last critical week—rightfully so, as the Cross and the Resurrection are the centerpiece of human history. These events prove the character of the Kingdom that Jesus has been declaring, this Kingdom in which the last will be first, the simple receive God's wisdom, servants are lifted up, and life can be found only by taking up a cross and dying. The values of this Kingdom are a radical contradiction to the values of this world, and the Messiah's victory-by-death proves it.

The Gospel of Matthew ends with all authority over heaven and earth in the hands of Jesus. With that authority, He gives His disciples a sacred assignment to complete before He returns. They are to be emissaries of the Kingdom among all peoples, not just within Israel. But they aren't just messengers; they are integral partners in His agenda. They are to go in His name, in His authority, and in the power of His presence, and He promises to be with them, even until the end of the age.

That's our mission too. Many reduce it to fulfilling an assignment to share a message or pass on information, but it's bigger than that. Our mission isn't just about telling and teaching; it's about living in the power of the Resurrection and the authority of the One who holds the keys of the Kingdom. It's experiencing Jesus' presence to the degree that others sense it in us. Just as Jesus' message was embodied in His lifestyle, so it should be with us. We aren't just to tell the Good News; we are to live it out. When we do, people are drawn into the Kingdom because they see the King who is with us.

## QUESTIONS FOR REFLECTION

In what ways are the values of Jesus' Kingdom radically different from the values of this world? How difficult is it to live by Kingdom values while we live in the world? How can we embody the Good News?

DAY 60

# MARK

Mark devotes eight verses to John the Baptist and then launches directly into Jesus' ministry. Within two chapters, Jesus has gathered disciples, stated His purpose (He has come for sinners, not for the righteous), demonstrated His authority over all kinds of diseases, and claimed lordship over the Sabbath itself—which stands for the entire law of God. This fast pace continues throughout the Gospel, which seems intent on presenting Jesus' credentials not so much through His teachings but through His works of power. It is action oriented; Mark uses the word *immediately* quite often to indicate that Jesus performed great works in rapid succession. It doesn't take long to find out that Jesus has authority over demons and storms—the most frightening aspects of the spiritual world and the most frightening natural occurrences. He can cleanse lepers and talk back to religious leaders. He even heals Peter's mother-in-law. He is the answer to every physical and spiritual need we have.

This Gospel includes some of Jesus' teachings, but not many, which is interesting since its primary purpose is to call people to discipleship. What kind of discipleship is it that doesn't major on instruction? How can we follow Jesus without thorough explanations from Jesus about what He wants from us? Apparently Mark thinks we can follow Jesus simply by observing Him. This is discipleship based on emulating a lifestyle. It isn't just about learning new information or modifying our behavior. It's about embracing everything Jesus is—in real-life action. Jesus' followers are to watch Him and do what they see.

What we see in Mark are supernatural acts of mercy and compassion, as well as radical sacrifice. In Mark (as in Matthew and Luke), Jesus startlingly envisions Himself being killed in the empire's worst form of execution—crucifixion—and then urges His disciples to embrace a similar sacrifice for themselves. Surely they were confused when Jesus said, "Take up your cross, and follow me" (Mark 8:34). *We have a cross?* they must have wondered. Only in the decades that followed would they finally understand what He meant.

Jesus also wants His disciples to base their lives on radical faith. "Why are you afraid? Do you still have no faith?" He says to His disciples after a storm (Mark 4:40). "Don't be afraid. Just have faith," He tells one supplicant (Mark 5:36). "You faithless people! How long must I be with you?" He cries out (Mark 9:19). "Have faith in God. . . . You can pray for anything, and if you believe that you've received it, it will be yours," He urges (Mark 11:22, 24). He rebukes the disciples for not believing in His resurrection even after others had told them about it (Mark 16:14), but He responds well to those who believe as much as they can yet still struggle with doubt (Mark 9:24). He understands the difficulty we have with faith, and He is patient toward us. But He still strongly commands us to believe.

We can believe in Jesus because Mark and the other Gospel writers give us a compelling picture of His authority over everything. There is no problem that can enter our lives that He cannot deal with. There are no walls that can't be torn down, no wounds that can't be healed, no relationships that can't be repaired, no storms He can't calm, no holes He can't get us out of, no diseases He can't heal, no crises that are too big for Him, and no enemy He can't overcome. He is the One our souls long for and the One in whom we can fully believe.

## QUESTIONS FOR REFLECTION

In what situations do you need to hear Jesus say, "Don't be afraid—just believe"? Why is this command appropriate in almost every area of our lives? Why do you think God made faith such a necessary aspect of relating to Him?

## DAY 61

# LUKE: THE MINISTRY OF JESUS

Luke writes in the style of a Greek historian, which is to say he compiles information in much the same way a journalist would when writing a profile story on an important figure. He uses Mark as source material (as does Matthew), but implies that he has also investigated a number of other sources, interviewed eyewitnesses, and provided as orderly and accurate an account as he can. He begins at the beginning—with Scripture's most thorough birth story about Jesus. He provides glimpses into the lives of people hardly covered in the other Gospels: the parents of John the Baptist; Mary, the mother of Jesus; two witnesses to Jesus' messianic identity, who meet Him at His consecration at the Temple; the women who support Jesus' ministry; Zacchaeus, the tax collector; and others. Luke covers Jesus' authority over diseases and demons and nature, just as the other Gospels do, as well as His claims and the nature of His mission. And there are personal touches and unexpected emphases not found elsewhere.

One of those emphases is Luke's focus on the marginalized of society. Though the other Gospels also show Jesus' compassion for the poor, the sick, and the "unclean," Luke goes further to demonstrate that the Messiah has come for *everyone*. The prominent place of women and Gentiles in Jesus' ministry may not stand out to us today, but it would have to Luke's readers. While Matthew describes the mission of the King and the nature of the Kingdom, and Mark focuses on the King's authority, Luke gives special attention to the King's subjects—the outcasts and the defiled, sinners of the worst kind, Jews loyal to the hated Romans, dirty shepherds tending flocks out in the fields, even Samaritan lepers. A messiah figure would be expected to come from the religious elite, or at least to befriend them. But Jesus finds more faithfulness and affection among the "lower" strata of society, the ones neglected by the religious elite. The dregs, the riffraff, those on the periphery—these are ones Jesus elevates as Kingdom citizens of the highest order, not because they are poor and rejected and ignored, but because they believe and follow Him. Their hearts are fertile soil for the seeds of the Kingdom. They are prime examples of the difference between the values of God's Kingdom and the values of the world.

This is a distinction we must thoroughly embrace if we are going to be followers of Jesus. He sees people differently than we do. He sees the world differently. He sees eternity differently. We express our allegiance to Him while still trying to satisfy our souls with whatever the world offers. We measure people, even inside the church, by their past rather than their potential. We try to build ourselves up, forgetting that our prime example for what it means to be human showed us that the way up is down—in servanthood, humility, and sacrifice. If we weren't already so familiar with the Gospels, they would blow our minds and shatter our assumptions.

One other emphasis in Luke sheds light on the power behind Jesus' ministry (and by implication, the power that enables us to follow Him and embrace His ministry as our own). Luke mentions the Holy Spirit twice as often as any other Gospel, and he continues the theme in his next book, the Acts of the Apostles, which some aptly call "the Acts of the Spirit." The Gospel of Luke ends with Jesus promising the Holy Spirit to His followers, assuring them that they will be filled with power from heaven. We see that promise fulfilled in Acts, but the implication is that we can still see it today. In Luke, the Spirit fills John, Mary, Elizabeth, Zechariah, Simeon, and Jesus Himself. Jesus promises that God will give the Spirit to anyone who asks. The promise at the end of the book says to wait in expectation. The entire Gospel comes across as an implied invitation. This Kingdom power is available to all who believe.

## QUESTIONS FOR REFLECTION

How does following Jesus change the way we see people? How does it change the way we see the world?

 DAY 62

# LUKE: THE PARABLES OF JESUS

Matthew and Mark tell us about many of Jesus' parables, but Luke seems to have a special interest in this mode of teaching and the powerful truths that come out of it. If not for Luke, we would not know about the Prodigal Son, the Good Samaritan, the rich fool, or the beggar named Lazarus. These colorful stories contain some of Jesus' most profound teaching.

Many of these parables are told during the "travel narrative," a section of Luke's Gospel (chapters 9–19) in which Jesus is on the road to Jerusalem. Two of these parables are on persistence in prayer. In chapter 11, a man doesn't stop knocking on his neighbor's door in the middle of the night until the neighbor opens and gives him a loaf of bread; in chapter 18, a widow pesters an unjust judge until he gives her the justice she asks for. After the first parable, Jesus urges His followers to keep asking, knocking, and seeking in order to receive. With the second, He urges them to pray constantly and not give up. Though God is neither a sleepy neighbor nor an unjust judge, He nevertheless responds to the prayers of the persistent. Jesus is clear that we should not lose heart.

Likewise, Jesus tells several parables about misplaced priorities, particularly with regard to money. In chapter 12, a very successful farmer thinks only of building bigger barns and accumulating more wealth, not realizing that his life is about to end and that he has been investing himself in the wrong things. In chapter 16, a man who has lived in luxury hardly notices the beggar at his doorstep, apparently completely unfamiliar with the compassion of God. In the afterlife, his torment awakens him to his foolishness, but it's too late. He neglected God's truth and focused on his own comfort and pleasure in his life on earth. The consequences are tragic.

But Jesus hasn't come simply to encourage the poor. He has come to rescue those who are lost, the captives of a broken world. When the religious teachers complain that Jesus is hanging out with disreputable people, He gives them three pointed parables: one about a shepherd who leaves ninety-nine sheep to look for one that is lost; a second describing a woman who searches high and low for one missing coin; and most famous, the story of a father with two sons, one of whom lives recklessly and offensively but eventually returns home, and the other who pitches a fit when his father throws a "welcome home" party for the unworthy rebel. In all of these parables, we get glimpses of Jesus' mission and God's joy over restored people, but the parable of the Prodigal Son captures our imaginations at the deepest level with its vivid portrayal of the younger son's foolishness, the father's heart, and the older son's bad attitude. Like us, neither son really understands the father's love or his own sonship. Jesus' purpose for coming into the world was to demonstrate both and to make it possible for our relationship with our heavenly Father to be fully restored.

Apart from the meaning of Jesus' parables, there's a message in the fact that He told so many of them. The human heart learns best from stories. This is why God didn't hand us a theology text-book or a list of rules and regulations. He gave us a book full of real lives and real encounters with Him. Stories are powerful, and we retain them for years. This is why Jesus taught in parables, and why the message of the law and the prophets wasn't enough to change us. We need God incarnate, a real encounter with the Father who steps into our lives in real time. We need to see the truth, not just hear it. We need the Immanuel of the Gospels, the "God with us." We need to experience the actual, living Jesus. And according to Luke, we can.

## Questions for Reflection

How do Jesus' parables change the way we understand prayer? How do they change the way we see ourselves as God's children?

 DAY 63

# JOHN 1–12

It doesn't take long to realize that John is a different sort of Gospel. With echoes of Genesis in the very first words, it portrays Jesus as the eternal Son of God, the creative force behind the universe, the wisdom and light from which all things exist. Where other Gospels build this revelation of Jesus' identity into their story lines, John opens with it and goes even deeper with it. The result is a carefully compiled selection of teachings, events, and "signs" that explore the relationship between light and dark, seeing and believing, and the Father and the Son. Where has this Light come from, and where is He going? Who truly believes—and what evidence is true faith based on? Who is the true Son of the Father, and which witnesses testify to His identity? These are the themes that are masterfully interwoven in the words of John's Gospel.

Many familiar stories and characters are found only in John: Jesus' turning of water into wine at a wedding in Cana; Nicodemus, the Pharisee who comes to Jesus at night; a disreputable Samaritan woman who meets Jesus at a well; a chronic invalid healed at the pool of Bethesda; a woman caught in adultery; and a friend named Lazarus who dies and is raised back to life. These characters and the events surrounding them become the platform for discussions about who Jesus really is, and He issues seven "I am" statements that point to His unique role as God incarnate. He is the true bread from heaven, the light that has come into the world, the Good Shepherd, and so on. The most inflammatory of these statements is not about Jesus' role, but about His eternal nature: "Before Abraham was even born, I AM!" (John 8:58). This prompts a violent reaction from His opponents, but Jesus escapes unharmed.

The interaction between Jesus and His opponents gets much more theological in John than in the other Gospels, as well as much more personal. Jesus and the religious leaders question each other's paternity, with Jesus eventually calling them sons of the devil (John 8:44) and them suggesting He's demon possessed (John 8:48). Jesus has already said that He only does what He sees the Father doing (John 5:19), and later He portrays His relationship to the Father in the most intimate terms: "The Father and I are one" (John 10:30). This question of fatherhood and Jesus' origin bubbles up frequently in the dialogue, and John makes it clear that the answer lies in the truth that God has clothed Himself in human flesh. Nowhere else in Scripture is it more apparent that Jesus is God and worthy of worship.

In this picture of the Incarnation, we see a God who goes to the greatest length possible to reconnect with His people and draw them into deep, intimate fellowship with Him—a theme that will become the centerpiece of the second half of this Gospel. Jesus sets His deeper teachings on this truth even in the earlier parts of the Gospel: The work of God is that His people might believe in Him (John 6:29); His sheep hear His voice—He knows them and they know Him (John 10:4, 14); they will know the truth—which, He says, is actually Him—and the truth will set them free (John 8:32). This is the most intensely relational Gospel of the four, a deeper look into the heart of God.

It's no wonder, then, that many have used John as their entry point into the life of Jesus or into a more personal relationship with Him. Clearly the "God with us" of all the Gospels has come to be known and to cultivate a relationship with us; but John takes that relationship to another level. It begins with a new birth, by seeing God and life in a new light, by drinking His living water and eating His bread from heaven—and His body and blood. In other words, we become one with Jesus just as He is one with the Father. It's a relationship that goes deeper than we ever imagined.

## QUESTIONS FOR REFLECTION

In what ways is John the most intensely relational Gospel? What does it show us about God's desire to be known?

 DAY 64

# JOHN 13–21

The first part of John's Gospel takes us through the raising of Lazarus and the aftermath. Apparently raising someone from the dead is dangerous business. Or perhaps it was the claim about being the resurrection and the life that got Jesus in trouble. Either way, there are now plots to kill both Lazarus (to cover up the evidence) and Jesus (to silence the alleged blasphemies). Quite a few people have believed, and quite a few have chosen not to. Regardless, Jesus has not come to judge the world but to save it.

Chapter 13 opens with the controversy about Jesus at full boil, in the final week of His life, in seclusion with His closest followers. He demonstrates His role as a servant by washing their feet and tells them to have the same servant-hearted attitude toward each other. He predicts His betrayal by one of His twelve closest followers. And then He imparts some final words, in a discourse that is perhaps the richest and fullest in all of Scripture. This "sermon" is contained in chapters 14–16.

Most surprising, Jesus suggests that it's better for His disciples if He goes away. That way, He can send His Spirit to live within each of them. Because of this, they will do greater works than He has done. The Spirit will comfort them, counsel them, guide them into all truth, and tell them of things to come. He will be their source for inside information about God, the Kingdom, and the world. And this, somehow, will be more real to them—or at least more powerful—than the physical presence of Jesus among them.

While Jesus is gone, so to speak, He will be preparing a place for those who follow Him, just as a groom and his father prepare a place in the family home for the new bride. The intimate implications of this relationship are addressed from several angles as Jesus talks about His love, the Father's love, and His disciples' love again and again. Jesus is the true Vine (an allusion to Isaiah's image of Israel as God's vineyard), and His followers are branches that derive their life from Him. They must not just remain *with* Him, or live *for* Him, but be *in* Him. This is how the Father shows Himself to believers, how their prayers get answered, and how they bear fruit that lasts for eternity.

On a more sobering note, these followers—the bride, the branches, the lovers of God—will face intense opposition in the world, though Jesus is about to overcome the world. Even as Jesus declares victory over the prince of this world, He also suggests that this enemy will sift the disciple Peter like wheat. There's tension between the "now" and the "not yet" of victory, but Jesus' followers will overcome because He overcomes. The fullness of this victory is seen in Jesus' prayer to the Father (chapter 17), in which He asks for astounding things, such as sharing His glory with His followers and making them one with each other and with Him in the same way that He and the Father are one. There are deep mysteries in these words, as well as a degree of mystical union between the human and divine—a union that finds expression in Jesus and, according to His prayer, in those who love Him. In other words, we become organically one with Him, fully sharing His life. The Light that came into the world resides in the hearts of those who believe.

This is a relationship that few of us understand, but we are called to experience it anyway. Those who are born of the Spirit long for it and find their fulfillment in it. We may be tempted to water down the words of Jesus in John—perhaps from our need to explain and define, or perhaps because our actual experience doesn't measure up—but the words keep calling us deeper. They point to the inexhaustible opportunity of being connected with God Himself. And they show us how to draw from an entirely different source of life than we've experienced before.

## QUESTIONS FOR REFLECTION

What are the implications of being one with Jesus in our attitudes and emotions? in our actions? in our relationships? How can we draw our life from Him?

DAY 65

# ACTS 1–12

In the opening verses of Acts, Luke gives us the outline of the book in the words of Jesus before His ascension: "You will receive power when the Holy Spirit comes upon you. And you will be my witnesses, telling people about me everywhere—in Jerusalem, throughout Judea, in Samaria, and to the ends of the earth" (Acts 1:8). The very next chapter describes the coming of the Holy Spirit in power, and the progression of the story throughout the rest of the book follows the geographical expansion Jesus has predicted.

At the end of the Gospel of Luke, Jesus told the disciples to wait in Jerusalem, and Acts 2 dramatically explains why. The Spirit falls tangibly upon a gathering of Jesus' followers during the feast of Shavuot—Pentecost, in Greek—and after a bold sermon by Peter, three thousand are added to the number of believers. Immediately, the nascent church experiences the same power Jesus demonstrated, enabling miracles, powerful preaching, and attitudes and outlooks that transcend circumstances. They experience the same opposition Jesus encountered too—Peter and John are arrested after healing a cripple at the Temple but aren't intimidated by the authorities' warnings. In some cases, these early believers are divinely protected, as when some of the apostles are miraculously delivered from prison. In other cases, they suffer martyrdom, as when James the brother of John is executed. Still, nothing quenches the boldness of this movement, at least in its earliest stages.

The church faces several internal tests as well. A husband and wife lie about their own generosity and die immediately. A ministry of caring for widows creates division when leaders appear to be favoring local Jews over Greek-speaking Jews from other regions of the empire. In this case, the controversy creates an opportunity;

the leaders chosen to oversee this ministry step into something of an apostolic ministry of their own. Philip, for example, ends up not only preaching in Samaria and along the coastline, but also has a divine encounter with an Ethiopian, whom he introduces to the truth of Jesus. Another of these servants, Stephen, performs miracles and teaches powerfully until he is martyred by a group of Jewish leaders who conspire against him.

At this point, the story begins to transition from a plotline dominated by the disciple Peter to one dominated by Saul of Tarsus (later called Paul), whose dramatic conversion will advance the "ends of the earth" mission of Jesus. The story shifts from Jerusalem, Judea, and Samaria to lands beyond.

Perhaps the greatest hinge on which this shift swings is Peter's vision in which God tells him to go to the home of a Gentile seeker who supports Judaism. The Holy Spirit falls even on this household of Gentiles, which creates quite a controversy back in Jerusalem (as does the simple fact that Peter entered the home of a Gentile and ate with him). The controversy is manageable at this point, though it will erupt further when Paul's preaching results in the conversion of Gentiles who had never been interested in or even introduced to Judaism and its practices. In Peter's ministry, the groundwork is laid for a radical development that will change the course of history.

The key to understanding the events of Acts is given to us at the very beginning in the words of Jesus: "when the Holy Spirit comes upon you" (Acts 1:8). It is presented in the context of a question about the Kingdom and when it will arrive. Jesus notably does not correct the disciples' assumptions about the Kingdom itself, but only about its timing. The Holy Spirit is the means through whom the Kingdom will come, and He will accomplish it largely through God's people. Though much throughout church history has been attempted by human wisdom or human effort— we seem to have an endless capacity for coming up with our own strategies and methods—the power of the events in Acts comes largely from people who simply respond to what the Spirit is doing in their midst. They do have strategies at times, but usually only when the Spirit is clearly leading. They could not have anticipated where He would lead, nor did they need to. They simply followed and allowed themselves to be surprised.

That's not a bad way to live. Our relationship with the Holy Spirit is as vital now as it was then. We are at times unreasonably content with an intangible, imperceptible, even powerless belief that He is there—somewhere—when in fact He urges us to seek Him, wait for Him, and encounter Him personally. This is our priority, even if it means not moving forward when we want to. And even if it means being completely surprised at where He leads us.

## QUESTIONS FOR REFLECTION

How can we balance the need to make plans in our lives with the need to respond to the Holy Spirit's leading? How do we know when to change directions to follow Him? Why is it important to be empowered by the Spirit?

 DAY 66

# ACTS 13–28

As a group of men worship together—one translation describes it as "ministering to the Lord"—they hear an assignment from the Holy Spirit. They are to set apart Paul and Barnabas and send them on a mission to spread the message of Jesus. This seems to be the first ministry effort not based in Jerusalem—the men who are worshiping are part of the church in Syrian Antioch, far to the north near Asia Minor—and it signifies a shift both in the plotline of Acts as well as in the history of Christian missions. This effort will eventually reach freely beyond the structures of Judaism to win believers directly from the pagan world.

The key figure in these missions is Paul, formerly known as Saul of Tarsus—the young rabbi who stood by at the killing of Stephen and relentlessly attempted to quench the Jesus movement. An encounter with the living Jesus on the road to Damascus changes him, and he becomes just as zealous in advocating the gospel as he had been in opposing it. But when his strategy of preaching first in synagogues yields more opposition than converts, he starts preaching directly to Gentiles steeped in paganism. A controversy erupts. The church calls a "time-out" and meets in Jerusalem to discuss critical questions. Doesn't a person have to embrace the law of God in order to come to Him? If Jesus is the Jewish Messiah, doesn't believing in Him imply some degree of Jewishness on the part of the believer? If God is grafting Gentiles into the tree of Israel, shouldn't the grafted branches look something like the tree itself? These were all valid questions with solid scriptural evidence for a "yes" answer, but the experience of Paul and several others—Peter among them—was that the Holy Spirit of God seemed to be filling Greek pagans without regard to their knowledge of Jewish Scripture and practices. And if God Himself wasn't keeping them at arm's length, how could the church?

This is an irrefutable argument from experience. The church will continue to sort out these questions for decades (and even millennia) to come, but God has nevertheless put the Spirit of His Jewish Messiah into Gentiles unacquainted with Judaism. They will benefit much by learning the Hebrew Scriptures, and their practices will conform to those scriptures in varying degrees, but their relationship with Jesus is not based on their circumcision, their kosher diets, or their keeping of feasts and Sabbaths. It's based on His living presence inside of them in response to their faith. He can be trusted to work righteousness into them as long as they seek His will wholeheartedly.

James, the half brother of Jesus and leader of the Jerusalem church, agrees to let the Gentile missions continue freely, and Paul and his various companions will take at least two more extended missionary journeys over the next few years. So will others whom Luke doesn't tell us about. Pockets of believers spring up in Asia, Europe, and Africa. Even Paul's eventual arrest takes him to Rome, where he is able to preach before the empire's highest authorities. The book of Acts ends very much in the middle of the story. Peter and Paul are still alive, though perhaps not for long, and the gospel continues to spread unhindered in spite of obstacles and opposition. Luke seems to understand that his account is the first chapter in a story that will continue throughout history.

We still live in that story, though at times we've departed on some tangents from the priorities, passion, and perspectives we read about in Acts. Nevertheless, the desires of God continue to drive His people toward the fulfillment of His Kingdom. We face opposition, we have internal disputes, we wrestle with deep issues about His will, we demonstrate great strengths and great weaknesses, and we continue to press on to the ends of the earth, all the while growing in our understanding of how comprehensive God's agenda really is. And, as we're filled with the Holy Spirit, we don't lose heart. As long as we are led by Him, He accomplishes His purposes in us, through us, and for us.

## QUESTIONS FOR REFLECTION

How open are you to being surprised by the Holy Spirit's direction? In what ways has He reshaped your thinking in the past? How long does it normally take for you to adjust to Him?

DAY 67

# ROMANS 1–8, 12–16

When Paul writes his letter to the Romans, he addresses a church that he wasn't instrumental in founding and that he hadn't ever visited. That's quite a contrast from his other letters, which are written to people in cities where he had deeply invested himself and had many personal connections. He hopes to go to Rome one day. But in the meantime, he can only write to this community of Christians that was founded by someone else and apparently has questions that Paul feels he must address.

Many consider Romans to be Paul's most comprehensive theological statement, though it does leave out some significant themes covered in his other writings. At the heart of Romans is the issue of how grace and faith fit into a religion steeped in law—and not just any law, but the everlasting law given by the voice and hand of God Himself on Mount Sinai and reaffirmed by Jesus the Messiah (Matthew 5:17-20). If there is forgiveness and life in the death and resurrection of Jesus, what role does God's law play in our lives now? Where does sin fit into the picture for someone who is thoroughly immersed in grace? Does grace mean freedom to live however we want?

These are some of the questions Paul seeks to answer, and he does so in typical rabbinic style. He points out that God related to Abraham on the basis of faith alone, long before the law was ever given. In other words, law has never been the key to a relationship with God. And righteousness—well, what human being can claim to have it? Abraham himself was declared righteous not because he behaved perfectly—sometimes he clearly didn't—but because he believed what God had promised. Righteousness comes through faith.

So what do we do with the law—those commandments God said He would never revoke? Paul explains that we have died with Jesus and risen with Him, so the law has no claim on us. We have an entirely different life now, a life in the Spirit. Instead of obeying an external, objective truth, we are inwardly transformed. We don't love because we are told to; we love because that's who we are. We don't keep ourselves pure because purity is commanded; we're pure because it's our new nature. That's the ideal we're growing into at least, even if we still experience the old nature at times. We have to learn to "reckon" or "consider" or "count on" this new existence to be true. When we do—when we fully believe it and rely not on our external efforts but on the power working within us—we experience this new, supernatural life.

So does the law matter? Of course it does; that's not the issue. The issue isn't legalistic righteousness versus libertarian grace, as some superficially suggest. Through our relationship with the Holy Spirit, we internalize the law. Obedience becomes the spontaneous outflow of a transformed heart. We still behave righteously, but for an entirely different reason. Our human flesh can't do it. The Spirit within us can.

This is the heart of the Christian life. Law doesn't make us righteous, but lawlessness isn't the answer either. When we are born-again—born from above—the culture and character from above begins to grow within us. Paul gives us a portrait of the character and culture of the Kingdom in chapter 12, but only after he has pointed us to the source that can produce this lifestyle. Anyone who begins reading Romans in the "what to do and how to live" section will fail miserably if they haven't first discovered the power of new life in Christ, through His death and resurrection.

This life, as Paul has emphasized, begins with faith. The prime example of faith is Abraham, the man God called in the very beginning when He was establishing His people, His family, and ultimately His nation through whom all others would be blessed.

Against all hope, Abraham in hope believed. He was absolutely convinced God would do what He promised (Romans 4:18-25), and God said, "Yes, that's righteousness." This is the attitude with which we approach Jesus—and really all of life—and God makes the same statement over us. When we can embrace Him like that, something happens inside. "Rightness" begins to spring forth from within. We bond deeply with Him, which has been His purpose all along. And we are never the same.

## QUESTIONS FOR REFLECTION

Why is it necessary to consider ourselves dead and resurrected with Jesus—that is, for the Holy Spirit to be the source of life within us? How can we distinguish outward obedience produced by our own efforts to obey God from inward obedience produced by the transforming power of the Holy Spirit in our lives?

 DAY 68

# ROMANS 9–11

Many observers see Romans 9-11 as the "great parenthesis" in this monumental letter—a sidebar commentary that takes Paul away from his primary purpose in writing. Others see this section as the pinnacle of the letter, the climax of all Paul has been saying. It's not a parenthesis at all, but the answer to the question that has been on everyone's mind. After all, if these first-century Christians are proclaiming a gospel of salvation by grace through faith alone, and yet the centerpiece of God's written revelation to this point has been a codified law that will never pass away, what does one make of the previous two millennia of human history? What was all that business about from Abraham to Moses to David to the prophets? How do you get away with saying, after all these centuries, "Scripture doesn't mean what you think it means"? And if God's own chosen people aren't widely accepting this new-sounding doctrine, what happens to them? These questions may be peripheral points of theology to the modern Christian mind, but Paul's doctrines were shocking, paradigm-shattering scandals in the context of first-century Judaism. He has to explain. And central to his explanation is the issue of Israel.

In Romans 3, Paul posed some vital questions and gave clear answers: What's the advantage of being a Jew and being circumcised? There are many advantages, he declares (Romans 3:1-2). Are Jews better off then? No, not at all (Romans 3:9). Already in the space of a few verses, this is a very confusing stance, even an apparent contradiction, so in chapter 9 Paul launches into a fuller explanation. In essence, his letter to the Romans has been building up to this for some time. Though Christian doctrine may sound new, it's rooted in Hebrew Scripture even more deeply than the law of Moses—in Abraham, his faith, and his calling. God's plan from the beginning was bigger than Israel. It is the firstborn nation (Exodus 4:22), but not the only-born nation. Israel is the context in which God has revealed Himself, even through the days of Jesus. The giving of the covenant, the revelation of His glory, the stories and experiences that unveil His nature, the seeds of the Kingdom that will never end—all belong to the family and the nation God set apart.

But none of these end there. Even in the days of the Exodus and the wilderness, God grafted foreigners into the community of His chosen people. Even in the days of the kings and the prophets, foreigners came into the Kingdom of God, as was foretold. And the prophets looked forward to a time when all nations would know God. Why is this doctrine of grace through faith a surprise? Why is attraction of the Gentiles scandalous? And if God has really planted His nature inside of us, does this grace-by-faith doctrine really lower His standards? Not at all. Israel is still chosen, but most Israelites have rejected God's plan in Jesus. Others are being grafted in. God's promises are still true—there will be a time when Israel comes back to Him en masse. Despite various claims throughout church history, God has *not* rejected His people (Romans 11:1). Not a single word of God's promises will be broken.

This theme shows up throughout the New Testament precisely because it was such a big question for the early church. Paul addresses it in much stronger language in Galatians. In Ephesians, he insists that the new nature within us breaks down all barriers between us, including the barrier between Jews and Gentiles. The Kingdom of God has always included Israel, but it transcends it as well. And the definition of "Israel"—that is, the descendants of Abraham—is being reshaped (Romans 9:6-8).

What does this have to do with Christians today in lands far from Israel, both culturally and geographically? Well, read the headlines. The eyes of the world are still focused on a strip of land in the Middle East, and not because that land has been forsaken by God. Quite the contrary—His whole plan still involves that land. It's where the Messiah said He would return. But beyond that, consider that God always keeps His promises, even when it seems as if His plan has changed or His people have forsaken Him. He may discipline them, He may delay fulfillment to a future generation, He may rearrange circumstances and adapt the promise to fit them. But He doesn't make promises He doesn't keep. We can count on that—even if it takes all of history to fulfill them.

## QUESTIONS FOR REFLECTION

What promises are you waiting for God to fulfill? What encouragement does the letter to the Romans offer when you experience delays or when it seems as if God is not coming through for you?

DAY 69

# 1 CORINTHIANS

Paul wrote several letters to the Corinthians, two of which have been preserved in Scripture. Even a cursory look at the first letter explains why he communicates with them so much: They have a lot of issues. They live in a very diverse, cosmopolitan city, and the competitive nature of their culture affects the fellowship of the church. They are envious of each other; they are divisive about which teachers they follow; they strive to have the most impressive spiritual gifts; they boast; they sue each other; they have a high tolerance for immorality; they offend each other's consciences in matters of worship and idolatry; they treat their bodies and their marriages casually; and they even take the Lord's Supper with a self-centered attitude—the exact opposite of what the Spirit of Christ and the Lord's Supper are meant to accomplish. So Paul writes corrective instructions to this fellowship, sometimes using very strong words, reminding them that they are called to be holy (1 Corinthians 1:2). They are believers, after all; but they are immature believers with a lot of dysfunctional relationships.

The apex of this corrective letter is a passage considered by many to be the finest expression of love in all of Christian literature. Chapter 13 is quoted at weddings and printed on plaques throughout Christendom. It beautifully and poetically describes what love looks like and what it doesn't look like. It is patient and kind, but not jealous or boastful or proud or rude. It's forgiving and not easily irritated. It never gives up, never loses faith, always hopes, and always endures (1 Corinthians 13:4-7). Why must Paul write these things? Not because of any poetic impulse about the virtues of love, but because the Corinthians are having problems with pride, rudeness, unforgiving attitudes, and impatience with each other. If they learn how to love—not sentimentally, but in a healthy sense, with truth and grace—many of their dysfunctions will fade away. But they are too focused on their individual interests, even when pursuing spiritual virtues. They are like people who take pride in their humility or who can't wait to learn patience. They are living contradictions to the Spirit they claim to follow.

Many misunderstand this letter as a critique of those who seek spiritual gifts, but it isn't that at all. In fact, Paul urges his readers to zealously pursue spiritual gifts—even eagerly covet them—especially the gift of being able to speak prophetically about the things on God's heart (1 Corinthians 14:1). Far from being a warning against enthusiasm, it's a warning against spiritual pride and abuses. Christian spirituality isn't performance oriented, and it isn't a competition. That's a much-needed message in many churches today, where true devotion to God takes a backseat to the logistics and outward appearances of a worship service. That problem can show up at either end of the spectrum—meetings that serve as a chaotic showcase for various egos as well as those that are so highly orchestrated that a polished presentation becomes the highest virtue. Paul urges humble, sacrificial, enduring, patient love. In other words, our major focus as Christians is to build up one another, not ourselves.

At its heart, 1 Corinthians is a lesson in attitudes—those that bring healing and unity as opposed to those that create chaos and division. It ends with Paul's most thorough treatment of the resurrection of Jesus, in which he distinguishes between a natural life in the decaying world and an imperishable life in the Kingdom of God. In essence, he calls the Corinthians to embrace the victory of the Kingdom—in attitude, in lifestyle, in their pursuit of God, in everything—and invest themselves in eternity. He has already told them that love never ends. As those raised from the dead, they will live in this love forever—with God and with each other.

## Questions for Reflection

To what extent does love—the kind of love Paul describes in 1 Corinthians 13—resolve virtually all of the relational problems we have? Why is this kind of love so rare and so difficult to practice?

 DAY 70

# 2 CORINTHIANS

Apparently Paul wrote a strongly worded, tear-inducing letter to the Corinthians sometime after 1 Corinthians was written. Whatever anger he expressed in it—seemingly because his last visit there was greeted with accusations about his motives and rebellion against his leadership—has provoked such a sorrowful reaction in the church that Paul goes to great lengths to comfort them in 2 Corinthians. He tries to soothe their suffering while talking about his own. The result is a letter partly justifying his authority and apostleship, partly identifying with their feelings, and partly motivating them to further embrace the sacrificial life. It is a letter about sacrifice and sorrow for a purpose.

This letter contains many of Paul's finest metaphors. We are earthen vessels that demonstrate the power of God rather than human capabilities (2 Corinthians 4:7). We are ambassadors of Christ, reconciling the world to Him just as He reconciled us to God (5:20). We are new creations in Christ, the old having passed away and the new coming in full (5:17). We are farmers who sow plentifully in order to reap plentifully—cheerful givers in whom God delights (9:6-7). Mixed in with these profound metaphors are explanations of what Paul has suffered for the sake of the gospel and, coincidentally, for the sake of the Corinthians.

He has been pressed but not crushed, perplexed but not despairing, struck but not destroyed (4:8-9). He has been jailed, whipped, beaten, shipwrecked, famished, cold, and burdened (6:4-10). He even has a thorn in the flesh—either a physical ailment or a nagging adversary—that God has not removed in order to keep him humble (12:7-9). Why has all this happened? Because Paul has worked tirelessly, forsaken many of his apostolic rights, and seen inexpressible heavenly visions. In other words, he has suffered not because God is against him, as some may charge, but because God is working so powerfully through him that the enemy has opposed him vehemently and violently. It's as if Paul is saying, "I'm sorry I got so mad at you for questioning my call, but I'm still going to defend it passionately." He is confident in his authority.

In this place of confidence, Paul does not back down from his appeal for the Corinthians to give generously—not to his own ministry, but to other suffering believers. This fits his opening theme well: God has comforted him so that he can comfort the Corinthians, so that they can comfort each other as well as those in need. This culture of comfort helps believers everywhere endure the opposition they receive as ministers of a new covenant. Yes, the calling is difficult; yes, we may be tempted to lose heart; yes, we have to fix our eyes on what is unseen rather than what is seen; and yes, godly repentance involves great sorrow. But God's promises are "yes" in Christ, His power is made perfect in weakness, and our light and momentary afflictions are preparing us for an eternal glory we can scarcely comprehend. The cost of embracing this Kingdom is huge, but the benefits always far outweigh the costs.

In a sense, this forms a challenge to the Corinthians and to us today. Are we going to bail out because the road is rough, or will we press ahead and experience the joys and blessings of the Kingdom? Many of the Corinthians seem to have a ready-to-bail attitude, but Paul urges them forward in their acceptance of his message—the message of how God reconciles a hostile world to

Himself. The trials and tribulations along the way are only a minor nuisance. The destination is vastly greater than the obstacles.

This is the kind of vision that keeps us going. Without it, we lose heart. But living by faith and not by sight, as Paul urges, keeps us pressing into the calling we've been given. At the end of John 16, Jesus told His disciples that they would have trouble in the world, but not to worry, for He had overcome the world. Second Corinthians is a case study in that truth. When the passing world tries to quench the new creation, the new creation overcomes.

## QUESTIONS FOR REFLECTION

How do our current troubles produce an eternal glory in us? Why can we be confident that our weaknesses are not a hindrance to God's power working within us?

 DAY 71

# GALATIANS

Early in Paul's missionary work, he and Silas visited several cities in southern Galatia (in Asia Minor) and spoke to both synagogue attendees and Gentile crowds. Several communities of believers developed from these efforts, as did violent opposition to Paul personally. Controversy erupted when Gentiles became believers in Jesus without going through normal conversion processes first—proceeding from paganism to observer status as a "God-fearer," then being initiated into Judaism, and then believing in the Jewish Messiah. The jump from God-fearer to Messiah-believer had already made some waves when a Gentile named Cornelius and his household believed Peter's message about Jesus and the

Holy Spirit was poured out on the Gentiles. But straight from paganism to Christianity? That was too much for many. A council was convened in Jerusalem to deal with the matter.

Apparently, around the time of the council—whether soon before or within a few years after—false teachers came to the churches in Galatia and began teaching a different message than the one Paul had given. These teachers emphasized Jewish commandments, such as circumcision and kosher diets, as integral parts of obedience to God and therefore as integral parts of the Christian life. For them, the issue wasn't only what is required to be saved, but how one lives after salvation. Paul's vehement response gives us one of the New Testament's most passionate letters. Paul is irate that the Galatians are quickly deserting the message he has given them. They began in the power of the Spirit; how can they continue in human effort? Any message that diverts them from a Spirit-saturated life, he says, even if it's delivered by an angel, is worthy of a curse.

In the course of his argument, Paul reveals a lot of personal information about himself. This is where we learn about his time in Arabia after his conversion, of his initial relationships with Peter and James, of his bitter controversy with Peter when Peter behaved one way around Gentile Christians and another to appease Jewish Christians, and of the general timeline of his early ministry. But more than that, we learn of the intensity of Paul's convictions about the relationship between law and grace. As a devout Jew, he never directly criticizes the law, but he certainly sees the means to fulfilling it far differently than his non-messianic peers. His criticism of the Judaizers—the ones who were insisting on bringing Jewish ceremonial law into Gentile faith—raises thorny issues. In the law itself, for example, God is emphatic that circumcision is to be a sign forever among His people. Yet Paul says it means nothing. What counts is a new creation (Galatians 6:15). As in Romans, we see the law internalized and spiritualized, and it doesn't look like the external law we're familiar with. This volatile topic comes up again and again throughout Paul's ministry.

We can be grateful for that because it gives him plenty of opportunity to explain how the Christian life is to be lived, particularly in that subtle distinction between life in the flesh and life in the Spirit. While most of us try to overcome the work of the flesh in the strength of the flesh, Paul says if we simply live by the Spirit—presumably ignoring the flesh completely—the fruit of the sinful nature won't be an issue. Living by the Spirit makes the law a nonfactor. The Spirit will produce in us virtues such as love, peace, patience, and joy (Galatians 5:16-25).

Even so, many people attack the old nature and try to get rid of it. This is not a fruitful lifestyle. Neither is trying to focus on all the details of righteousness. Our entire focus is to be on our love for and relationship with God—in Jesus, through His Spirit. When He thrives within us, we have intimacy with Him and He produces whatever He wants to produce in us. That's the gospel. That's the simplicity of the message. Anything else, according to Paul, leads us away from life.

## QUESTIONS FOR REFLECTION

What is the difference between living by the Spirit and living by the flesh? Why don't we need to worry that living by the Spirit instead of the law will lead to unrighteousness?

DAY 72

# EPHESIANS

Ephesus was the third-largest city in the Roman Empire and a center of pagan devotion and the practice of magical arts. Paul spent about three years there, and the rise of Christian influence in the city created a lot of tension, especially between Christians and the people who made money in and around the temple of Artemis. Their religious tourism trade—amulets, goddess figurines, incantation scrolls, astrological readings—was suffering, and their protests to the guild prompted a riot against Paul, who promptly left town for the sake of the Christians there. The churches in the area continued to grow in spite of the opposition, and now Paul is writing them a letter to encourage them.

He uses the language of the city in this letter, referring to powers and principalities, mysteries and enlightenment, and love that surpasses any spiritual knowledge a person can acquire. He refers to the power of Jesus in epic terms, just in case any of his readers might be wondering where He fits in comparison to other gods. He never denies the hierarchy of spiritual beings that lurk in the consciousness of some people; he simply points out that Jesus is seated high above all of them. Not only that, he tells them that they are seated with Jesus in the highest heavenly realms and can put on a set of spiritual armor that will protect them from true spiritual danger, presumably far better than any incantation or amulet is able to do. His words imply the vast superiority of Christian truth over the pagan culture without directly confronting the pagan culture. This is a gospel of greater power, deeper wisdom, and higher potential.

Ephesians contains powerful prayers that we can pray for each other and expect profound results (Ephesians 1:17-19; 3:16-19).

It presents a beautifully condensed summary of the plan of salvation (Ephesians 2:1-10), which begins with our utter hopelessness and ends with our exaltation with Christ as evidence of God's workmanship in and through us—by grace through faith alone. It gives us instruction on relationships, including a portrayal of marriage as a picture of Jesus and His bride. It describes our new life in Christ in terms of taking off old clothes and putting on new ones. It presents spiritual gifts as spoils of Jesus' victory and a key to building us up into His fullness. And it addresses the ever-present Jewish-Gentile question, declaring the wall between them obsolete.

These are sweeping themes, and we've spent the last two millennia probing them. In fact, some of these words are so extravagant that we generally have a hard time believing them. For example, are we really blameless in God's sight (Ephesians 1:4)? Seated with Jesus in heavenly realms (Ephesians 2:6)? Filled with all the fullness of God (Ephesians 3:19)? Sometimes we look at our own lives and can see them falling far short of these lofty ideals. When we do, we have a couple of options: (1) explain Paul's concepts in words we can understand, which usually involves watering them down somewhat; or (2) continue to go deeper, reach higher, and press in to God for the fullness He offers. The first option helps us resolve things intellectually, but is ultimately unsatisfying. The second can be frustrating in the process, but is ultimately rewarding. Our choice reveals a lot about how much we hunger for God. It helps to hang on to the truth of Ephesians 3:20—that God is able "to accomplish infinitely more than we might ask or think." Scripture calls us to enormous impossibilities, yet repeatedly tells us that nothing is impossible. Faith—itself a gift of God, according to Ephesians 2:8—can deal with that mystery and lead us into God's most lavish blessings.

## Questions for Reflection

Why is it hard to believe extreme statements about our life in Christ—such as our being seated with Him in heavenly places or being filled with God's fullness? How can we experience these truths in practical ways?

 DAY 73

# PHILIPPIANS

Philippians is a very emotional letter. Some people think emotions have little to do with our spiritual lives, but Paul—the man whose zeal shows up in Galatians, whose sorrow shows up in 2 Corinthians, and whose joy shows up in Philippians—would disagree. In fact, Paul fills his letter to the church in Philippi with emotive words such as *joy, love, longing, tender compassion,* and *eager expectation.* He counsels them about jealous ambition and anxiety. And he even encourages them at one point to let their minds line up with the way they feel (Philippians 2:1-2). His words overflow with affection.

That's quite a contrast to some of Paul's other letters, where his anger and passion come across almost harshly. The church in Philippi causes him less pain than the others because they seem to have the fewest issues. They have sent him a monetary gift, apparently while he's under house arrest in Rome, and he is grateful. But he is also instructive, as is his nature, and speaks truth into a couple of their minor problems. They are dealing with a quarrel between two women of influence, and they are apparently overly concerned about that and other issues. Paul urges peace, both in relationships and in their hearts. They have no real reason to be anxious, because God will answer every prayer they offer in faith and gratitude. They can focus on whatever is good and true and beautiful, knowing that hearts filled with these things are inhabited by God's fullness and peace. They can serve one another in humility, knowing that God honors servant-hearted people with His blessings. God is working in them and will continue to do so until His work is complete. They have nothing to worry about.

Even so, Paul points out a few specific situations that could cause them to worry if they were so inclined. His imprisonment and impending sentence, for example, are causes for concern, as well as those who are preaching from their own ambition while he is in prison. There are also false teachers around, people who put confidence in their own ability to be godly and who surround themselves with the trappings of true faith—just as Paul used to do with his Jewish heritage and devotion. But all these things are rubbish compared to intimate fellowship with Jesus. Dying is actually *gain* in God's Kingdom, and Paul is ready for that. There are the minor grumblings within their fellowship that, if left unchecked, could turn molehills into mountains. Paul reassures them about all of these things, insisting that pure joy is possible in the midst of everything because joy runs much deeper than circumstances.

The pinnacle of this letter is an early hymn about Jesus that Paul includes as a case study in having the right attitude (Philippians 2:5-11). Jesus Himself showed what true servanthood is like. He emptied Himself of the privileges of deity in coming to earth as a human and sacrificing His own life for others. This is what Paul means by having a selfless attitude. He can do more than simply describe it; he gives them a visual example. And if his readers wonder if this kind of life is rewarding, all they need to do is look at how God exalted Jesus. He has been given the highest place in heaven and earth and a name above all names. Everyone will eventually acknowledge His lordship. Jesus poured out His life; Paul is in the process of pouring out his own life; and the Philippians should be doing the same. The rewards are unimaginable.

Philippians is a great source of spiritual sound bites—don't be anxious, do all things through Christ, God will complete the work He began in us, and so on. But it's more than that. It's a message on the joy that's found in selflessness and humility. Humble sacrifice isn't the most appealing message at certain times in our lives, especially when we're looking for specific encouragement about our circumstances. But it's the most rewarding. And it's the only way to have true joy in the Lord and peace that passes understanding.

## QUESTIONS FOR REFLECTION

How can we have joy in all circumstances? How can we have peace in trying times? What will humility accomplish in our relationships with God and with others?

 DAY 74

# COLOSSIANS

No one today knows exactly what false teachings were spread in Colossae, but we know how Paul responds to them. From what he writes, we can tell that the false teaching somehow minimized the role of Jesus in the lives of believers and magnified the threat of spiritual powers. It also magnified the effectiveness of ascetic practices—extreme self-denial of physical pleasures—and of ritual behavior related to feasts and Sabbaths. In other words, the people in the Colossian church had somehow been led to overemphasize their own spiritual power and underemphasize the power of Jesus.

What the believers in Colossae don't seem to understand is

that focusing on one's own spiritual abilities and efforts inevitably has the opposite effect of what one wants. For example, trying to escape corruption and become pure through self-discipline is putting confidence in the very flesh that was weak and ineffective to begin with. In trying to become spiritual, they are placing faith in their own efforts. That's utter futility.

Instead, Paul points them to Jesus, the image of the invisible God. Jesus is above all things. Everything was created by Him and for Him. He is the heir of all that belongs to God, the head of the church, and the One in whom God fully dwells. Not only that, but He has already delivered us from the kingdom of darkness—there's nothing left for us to do on that issue. He has already canceled our debt toward God and, in the process, defeated and shamed all spiritual powers that oppose God and His Kingdom. He has raised us from the dead and given us supernatural life. As a result, we share in the inheritance of the Son.

This is enough. We don't need to attain a higher level of spirituality by our own efforts. We don't need to gain power over spiritual powers of darkness because we already have it. We don't need to be captivated by elaborate philosophies or holy-sounding traditions. We shouldn't let anyone judge us on how well we practice feasts and Sabbaths. These things are shadows of reality, not the substance. The substance is Jesus, and we already have Him in full.

Colossians reminds us that there's a lot of spirituality in the world that appears to be pure and wise and noble, but is essentially empty. This is especially true of spiritual teachings that emphasize what we do rather than what Jesus has done. These teachings are ineffective. That applies even to God's own standards—Paul argues elsewhere that the law never accomplished righteousness for anyone. Whenever we turn to a system of belief or spiritual practices or human traditions, we are investing ourselves in powerless solutions.

What are we to do instead? Set our minds on the things above, not the things on earth (Colossians 3:2). More specifically, we are to fix our gaze on Jesus Himself. He is the One who overcomes the things that defeat us, who gives us fullness deep within, who makes us pure down to our very core, and who holds power over every spirit. There is no problem we can encounter—spiritually, emotionally, or physically—that He cannot overcome. When we fix our focus on Him and not on the corruptions and weaknesses and failures that we've tried so hard to overcome, those issues fade into the background. We overcome them not by focusing on them but by focusing on a much greater power. Our effort takes a backseat to His effort, and the results are much more fruitful.

## Questions for Reflection

How does setting our minds on things above and fixing our eyes on Jesus accomplish what we need spiritually? How does this approach to spiritual growth help satisfy God's desire for closeness with us?

 DAY 75

# 1 THESSALONIANS

The return of Jesus was a major theme in the teachings of the early church, and for most people, it was an encouraging one. But when some believers died, it caused considerable alarm and grief. After all, how can someone participate in the Kingdom of God if he or she dies before Jesus comes back to set it up? Somehow the believers in this church developed false assumptions about the end of the age and God's timing. So Paul lovingly corrects them in this letter, reassuring them that when Jesus returns, those who have died and those who are still alive will be caught up together to meet Him.

Even so, the return of Jesus has some strong implications for those who are alive. He is coming for a pure people, so we must get rid of all impurity. He is coming to establish justice, so we should never take advantage of others. He is coming like a thief in the night, so we must live with a sense of readiness. In matters of ethics and morality, there's no dilemma in these instructions; it's always appropriate to be pure and just. But in the expectation of the heart, this posture between being ready and waiting can create a lot of tension. Here Paul tends to emphasize the possibility of Jesus' return being soon, whereas in his second letter to the Thessalonians, he must remind them that it could seem slow in coming and that certain signs must occur first. This tension appears at times throughout the New Testament, and we still see it today when non-Christians scoff at the very idea of Jesus coming back, while Christians wait expectantly for Him. Jesus' Second Coming is a solid doctrine in Scripture, but it's shrouded in mystery. Even Jesus told His disciples He didn't know when it would be.

First Thessalonians covers other issues as well, notably Paul's defense of himself in light of accusations that he didn't care for the church or had selfish intentions in his relationship with it. He hadn't visited in a while, so how invested was he in this group of believers? Paul talks about his longing to see them, describes how he wanted to come once but Satan thwarted him, and implies that Timothy's presence qualifies as a visit from the apostolic team. In other words, he is not an absentee apostle, one who's neglecting his charges. Rather, his thoughts are often with them and his affection for them is as strong as ever.

The other significant issue in this church involves people who aren't working, perhaps because they depend on the wealth of generous Christians or because they are simply lazy. Regardless of the reason, Paul urges them all to be industrious and earn their own income. This theme is expanded in Paul's next letter, but the need for instruction is present early on. In this new community based on generosity and sharing of resources, especially in times of persecution when everyone bands closely together, some people pull more weight than others. It's important for everyone to contribute selflessly.

The letter ends with a powerful sequence of statements. First, one of Scripture's most succinct, compelling, and diverse set of instructions is packed into 1 Thessalonians 5:16-22: "Always be joyful. Never stop praying. Be thankful in all circumstances. . . . Do not stifle the Holy Spirit" (verses 16-19). Then comes one of Scripture's most encouraging promises, after an exhortation to be blameless: "God will make this happen, for he who calls you is faithful" (1 Thessalonians 5:24). This promise applies not only to the impossibility of being fully pure as His coming approaches; it also applies to anything else God calls us to do. His equipping, His power, and His opportunities will always accompany His leading. That can be a winding, lengthy process, but it's also a certain one. God accomplishes what He begins.

## Questions for Reflection

How does our hope for Jesus' return shape how we live now? What does it mean for our work? our purity? our long-term relationships?

 DAY 76

# 2 THESSALONIANS

Paul wrote another letter to the Thessalonians soon after he wrote the first one, a rarity that would only be necessary if something had suddenly happened to change the church's situation. From Paul's response, only one explanation makes sense: It seems that someone, apparently in a forged letter claiming to be from Paul, had convinced the church that Jesus had already returned. The Thessalonian believers are greatly alarmed, of course, since being unaware of His coming means being left out. But Paul reassures them that Jesus has not come back yet, and that there are certain signs that must happen before He will. He cryptically describes a time of rebellion, a man of lawlessness, and a restrainer who is keeping lawlessness from being fully revealed. Even though Paul and his companions have performed true signs and wonders among the Thessalonians, Satan will deceive many with false signs and wonders. In the midst of this, the believers are to stand firm and not be moved. The fact that they have lived fruitfully and shown evidence of the Spirit is proof enough that they will not be left out when Jesus comes. He has come to save His people, not to ignore them.

The misperception about Jesus' return seems to have made a couple of the Thessalonians' problems worse. They may be interpreting their recent persecution as evidence of God's judgment rather than as a sign that they are on the right track and drawing the same kind of opposition Jesus experienced. Paul assures them that their endurance is actually evidence of their salvation and that God will eventually judge their enemies harshly. The other problem is that those who have not been working diligently to earn their own income seem to be justifying their laziness by the fact that Jesus has already come. And if He hasn't, He probably will soon, they reason. So why work hard in such urgent times? This logic has surfaced at various times throughout church history and has always proven harmful. Unlike Martin Luther, who is said to have remarked that he would plant a tree today even if he knew the world would end tomorrow, many people stop building for the future when they think they see the final day approaching. We can assume from Paul's words and other scriptural instructions that Jesus would rather see us busy than idle when He returns.

We need to remember that, in any prophetic prediction or promise, the substance of what God has said is certain, but the timing is rarely specified. Scripture is full of people who received a vision or calling from God and waited long years for it to come to pass. He will do what He said He would do, but not necessarily when we expect Him to. We try to figure out His timing—it's almost irresistible to try to pin it down—but we're usually wrong. That's the case in personal matters that unfold over the course of a lifetime and even more so in ultimate matters that unfold over the course of history. No matter how many signs point to Jesus' return, we still won't know when it will be until it happens. Neither will we see His promises to us fulfilled exactly when we expect them. But we *will* see them fulfilled.

This is why patience is a key virtue in God's Kingdom. His timing is different from ours. Because His purposes are thorough, His plans sometimes unfold very slowly. When He acts, it may seem sudden to us, but it's usually after years of preparation that we haven't seen or understood. Until the time of fulfillment, God works almost imperceptibly. In the process, He builds our faith and trust. We have to hang on and endure.

That's what Paul tells the Thessalonians. Hang on and endure. Don't lose heart. Don't believe lies that say the time of fulfillment has passed. Don't make assumptions about God's timing. Watch for the signs and wait expectantly. His purposes will be fulfilled in due time.

## QUESTIONS FOR REFLECTION

How can we balance being ready for Jesus' return with being responsible in planning for the future? Why is patience such an important attribute in God's Kingdom?

DAY 77

# 1 TIMOTHY

When Paul left Ephesus for Macedonia, he left Timothy behind as a voice of truth to stand against false teaching. Now he writes a letter to encourage Timothy and advise him more specifically about some of the controversies his young protégé faces. He reminds Timothy of some prophetic words that were spoken over him. If he will cling to these, they will keep him focused on his calling and help him fight the good fight. Timothy is called to remain grounded in the midst of swirling, dizzying debates.

Much of this letter is filled with practical pastoral advice. What qualifies someone to be a church leader? How does one distinguish between people—particularly widows—who are truly in need and those who aren't? How does one live faithfully in the midst of hypocrisy? These questions are relevant in any age, but many wonder whether Paul's answers are still timely. He does make some rather controversial statements about women, though saying that these are his own policies. Are they God's, too? Are they specific to the culture of Paul's day or universal truths? Without knowing the precise context in which they were given, is it possible to know exactly what Paul meant by them? Christians continue to debate these things, sometimes humbly and with balance, sometimes with the kind of nitpicky detail and legalistic zeal Paul condemns elsewhere in 1 Timothy and in other letters. Whether Paul gave his pastoral instructions—not only about women but also about church leaders and other ministry issues—as unbreakable laws or as fatherly advice is the subject of much division in the church, a situation Paul surely would have wished to avoid.

In all of his letters, Paul seems vehement about the doctrines that matter most—the nature of God and Jesus, the means to salvation, and the inspiration of Scripture—and very impatient with speculations and nonessential details. He speaks with contempt about hypocrisy, legalistic requirements, philosophical musings, pointless myths, unhealthy quarrels, constant friction, and divisive people. He frequently points his readers back to the simplicity of salvation—Jesus did it all and birthed His life within us. Doctrinal controversies apparently raged in nearly every church at some point in the first century, which only makes sense when a movement is trying to sort out what God has done and what His work means for His purposes for the world and humanity. But would Paul engage in the endless theological nitpicking that often goes on today—trying to figure out all the mysteries of God while neglecting the actual practice of relevant ministry? Probably not. He is always focused on the core of the faith. God's people are called to unite around the essentials and refuse to divide over the details.

The issues in Paul's letters to Timothy reveal that church life in the first century was as messy as it is today. Any diverse group of human beings includes multiple backgrounds, needs, agendas, opinions, and perspectives. Sorting them out can be a process. But Paul's advice to Timothy about remembering the prophecies spoken over him, which reminded him of his calling, are critically important. We can't stay focused on our purpose if we forget how God has led us in the past and what He has promised to do through us. We easily get distracted with issues and opinions that divert us from the simplicity of our devotion to Jesus. We turn our faith into something exclusively mental, exclusively emotional, or exclusively practical, forgetting that it's about the reality of the living Jesus inside of us, moving us and leading us moment by moment rather than simply giving us policies and procedures to follow. We can only fight the good fight when we hang on tightly to the eternal life that God has given us (1 Timothy 6:12). The gospel is living truth, not a discussion of doctrine. And that's worth contending for.

## QUESTIONS FOR REFLECTION

Do you think some Christians and churches today divide over distracting details and get caught up in pointless arguments? Why or why not? What do you think are the essential beliefs Christians must agree on?

DAY 78

# 2 TIMOTHY

While under house arrest in Rome, Paul writes Timothy another letter and asks him to come and visit. This letter is much more personal and less down-to-business than Paul's previous correspondence with Timothy—less about Timothy's role as a church leader and more about his spiritual·growth. The familiarity and tenderness in this letter is unique; Paul's other writings are to groups of people or to friends who aren't quite as close. With Timothy, he is more interested in sharing his heart than in passing on instructions.

This tone gives us some rare glimpses of the apostle. He writes with sadness about those who have deserted him, some who are ashamed of his status as a prisoner in Rome. Perhaps this is one reason he laments that only Luke is with him and invites Timothy to come. The bold Paul even asks the timid Timothy not to be ashamed of him, declaring that he isn't ashamed of himself because he knows whom he has believed. And because Timothy has not been given a spirit of fear, he need never be ashamed of his testimony. This verbal interplay between confidence and shame is revealing—as if Paul realizes how disreputable his arrest and long imprisonment must appear to other believers and to the outside world. But it's still a necessary result of his ministry. He doesn't apologize for it, but he does understand its impact on the churches he founded. And he wants to make sure his situation doesn't add to Timothy's apparent insecurities.

Though the purpose of the letter isn't instructional, Paul still has some advice for Timothy. He wants his young friend to train like a soldier and an athlete and wait like a farmer—to be focused, persistent, and patient. He should entrust the truths of the gospel to reliable people who can share the load in teaching and training others. As Paul says in his first letter, Timothy would do well to avoid pointless quarrels and foolish discussions, presenting himself instead to God as someone who can handle the Word of Truth responsibly. This is especially important for the Lord's servants, who must be patient with even the most difficult people and gently teach those who disagree with them. Proving a point isn't as important as displaying the right character in the discussion.

Finally, Paul warns Timothy about impurity and reminds him of the corruption of the last days. People will be proud, greedy, disobedient, ungrateful, and ignorant of all that is sacred. Practically any generation can apply this description to its own people, but that's not the point. The point is to understand the lure of a profane culture and avoid its trappings. That's what Paul has done, and now he can confidently say that he has fought the good fight, is finishing the race, and is looking forward to the reward. He sees the end, and he is ready for it.

This is the perspective we all want to finish with. It's an echo of Jesus' statement that He had accomplished all that the Father had given Him to do (John 17:4). Paul could have nurtured regrets about his pre-Christian life, but he focused instead on what he was able to accomplish with the grace he had been given. We can do the same, putting our failures behind us and investing our lives in the things that will last forever. Regrets are unnecessary in a kingdom of grace and restoration. We are not like autumn leaves that are blown away by the wind, but rather like spring seeds that grow up into fruitfulness. We can let go of any bitterness about missed opportunities and zealously pursue the ones God puts before us now. If we are running our race and fighting our fight with the grace we have been given in the moment, God is pleased. When we get to the end, we too will receive the crown of righteousness that is given to those who await Jesus' return.

## QUESTIONS FOR REFLECTION

How do the illustrations of a soldier, an athlete, and a farmer help us stay focused on what's most important? Why do we need to eliminate distractions in our spiritual lives?

 DAY 79

# TITUS

In contrast to 2 Timothy, Paul's letter to Titus is direct and businesslike—a very straightforward expression of apostolic authority. Paul had recently started churches in Crete and left Titus behind to lead them, but false teachers have crept in quickly. The presence of distorted beliefs is serious in any situation, but especially among new believers who aren't well-grounded. Titus's job—and the job of the elders he chooses to appoint—is to ground them in truth. Paul describes the character of godly elders, who need to be the kind of men who aren't easily swayed or tempted. False teaching can be effectively countered by stable people who lead the congregation.

No one today knows the exact nature of the false teaching infiltrating the church. As in Colossae, it seems to have been some peripheral strain of Judaism that involved myths, legalistic practices, and endless discussions. Regardless of the details, its proponents emphasized purity with their words, but didn't practice it with their lives. This seems to have been popular in a place like Crete, which Paul says has a well-deserved reputation for corruption. In any culture, it's easy to claim to know God and then live as the culture dictates. That's what the false teachers seem to be doing. Paul says their actions aren't consistent with their words. They deny God by their lifestyle and are leading others to do the same.

This is why Paul's description of the character of church leaders is important, as is his encouragement for older men and women to train younger men and women in matters of life and faith. In fact, the whole letter seems to emphasize the practical aspects of the Christian life—how we live in response to what God has done and the life He has put within us. Like the rest of Paul's letters, it never tells us how we should behave without first describing the source of our life. Inner transformation comes first, then actions. Any gospel that focuses on outward behavior is no gospel at all. It isn't good news to command the old nature to live like the new one—it's thoroughly frustrating. Only when we are reborn with a new nature can we live new lives.

Paul gives us great summaries of the gospel in Titus 2:11-14 and 3:3-6, passages that prioritize the new creation inside—the new life we have by grace through faith—but that also emphasize doing what is right. We aren't just made righteous when Jesus returns; we demonstrate godliness now. As a tree bears fruit according to its species, actions manifest in our lives according to the nature within us. Inner transformation always has outward evidence. We are united with God after all. It has to make a difference.

The truth of Jesus therefore applies to our relationships, our ethical behavior, our attitudes, our work habits, our finances—everything. We can't compartmentalize our lives into sacred and secular divisions, with one side set apart for spiritual devotion and the other for practical behavior. If Jesus is real in one area, He must be real in all of them. God did not rescue parts of us; His rescue plan involves body, soul, spirit, and everything else that is broken. Even today, many Christians clearly see the spiritual side of salvation without understanding its fullness. And many embrace an understanding of the truth without any desire to live it. Scripture gives us no such option. God's desire is to invade every aspect of our hearts, minds, and actions. He wants a relationship with our whole being. Anything less falls short of the hope and glory He has promised.

## QUESTIONS FOR REFLECTION

Are there any ways in which you're tempted to compartmentalize your life and leave God out of certain aspects of it? If so, what can you do to embrace a fuller, more holistic salvation?

 DAY 80

# PHILEMON

At some point in his ministry, Paul introduced a man in Colossae to Jesus. This man, Philemon, had become a church leader, hosting a congregation in his family's home. Years later, Paul is under house arrest in Rome and has somehow come in contact with a runaway slave named Onesimus, who is probably trying to remain unnoticed in the large city. Paul introduces this slave to Jesus, too, and becomes his "father" in the Lord. Onesimus is potentially very useful to Paul—able to attend to his many needs—since prisoners were required to supply their own food, lodging, and other necessities while under Roman guard. A friend to run errands is always helpful for someone in confinement. But Paul understands that Philemon has lost a servant, as well as any money or goods the servant took with him. The right thing to do is send Onesimus back to his owner.

For Onesimus, this would mean not only swallowing his pride, but also risking his life. Philemon could technically press to have Onesimus executed because it was a serious crime for a slave to run away from his or her owner. But Paul appeals to Philemon's sense of forgiveness. As an apostle, he could try to command Philemon to do the right thing, but he chooses not to go that route. He reasons with Philemon and promises to take responsibility for any losses Philemon has suffered—probably knowing that Philemon will charge absolutely nothing to Paul's account because he already feels eternally indebted to him. Paul recommends a solution and fully expects Philemon to accept it.

Paul could have chosen to address the evils of slavery at some point in his letters, but he doesn't—a bothersome fact for many people, and understandably so. But Paul was dealing with immediate relationships within a culture that wasn't about to change on that issue. He never addressed the rights and wrongs of Roman practices. Slavery was a fact of life. And it was more varied than we normally think. Some slaves were forced laborers who came from the spoils of war and subjugated peoples, but many more were voluntarily paying off debts with a designated term of service. We don't know which situation Onesimus was in, but we do know that both he and Philemon would have understood that his escape was unethical and illegal, evidence of a broken relationship.

Our relationship with Jesus transforms our relationships with others, at least ideally. Jesus told us to forgive as we have been forgiven, threatening severe consequences for those who receive God's enormous mercy and then withhold their own mercy for lesser offenses. Forgiveness is at the heart of the gospel, so much so that the story of Onesimus and Philemon can be seen as a living parable of the gospel itself. Someone under a potential death sentence is being forgiven by his master because a son of God intercedes for him and says to credit all debts to his account. That profoundly echoes the big-picture story, especially when the slave becomes a brother in Christ. This is the gospel in action.

It's significant that Paul sees Onesimus's mistake in light of God's sovereign purposes. Onesimus ran away illegally, but his rebellious path led him to Paul, and as a result, to eternal salvation. Now he's no longer a servant; he's much more, to both Paul and Philemon. Even in human failure, God has worked all things together for good (Romans 8:28).

That's the testimony of Scripture as a whole and of the letter to Philemon in particular. In the midst of brokenness, there's restoration. People are brought back together, offenses are covered, and God's love is poured out in every area of our lives. Neither the big-picture story nor our own personal story ends in limbo. God makes us and our relationships whole.

## Question for Reflection

In what ways is the story of Onesimus a picture of the gospel?

 DAY 81

# HEBREWS

Jewish believers have had a rough time. Some are in prison or have been otherwise mistreated (Hebrews 13:3). They have come face-to-face with hostile opposition from the religious leaders they once relied on and have realized that they are being marginalized from the culture of their heritage. Many of those leaders seem to have raised serious questions about Jesus; for example, how can He be the high priest from God if He isn't even a Levite? As a result, many are questioning their faith in Messiah and falling away from it, returning to the comfort and safety of their more traditional views. Some are still wavering or have simply grown weary and are now neglecting the teachings of Jesus and the fellowship of His people. There seems to be a tragically increasing exodus from this messianic movement.

The author of Hebrews—still unknown—sends a written sermon to these believers to encourage them to stay the course. He begins by emphasizing the uniqueness and superiority of Jesus. He isn't just an angel or a prophet or a human priest. He's the Son of God, the exact representation of the Father, the perfect reflection of God's glory. He came in the form of a human and a Jew, identifying with His people and their weaknesses, trials, and temptations, but He isn't like any priest they have ever known. It's true that He isn't a Levite, but the priesthood of Aaron had its limitations. Jesus comes from an altogether different priesthood, one represented by Melchizedek, the mysterious "king of righteousness" who appeared to Abraham, received his offerings, and shared with him a meal of bread and wine (see Genesis 14:18-20). This priesthood is eternal and perfectly holy, not like the priesthood that repeats sacrifices year after year in earthly Temple rituals, which are but shadows of heavenly realities. Therefore, this Messiah is the only one able to save.

The writer of Hebrews draws a parallel between the Jews who are currently being delivered by Jesus and those who were delivered from Egypt and rebelled in the wilderness. He warns them not to have the same evil heart of unbelief as their forefathers had in the desert. If that generation missed the Promised Land because of its lack of faith, and if Jesus offers the ultimate Promised Land, what deliverance is left for this generation if it falls away and neglects so great a salvation? There's no plan B. If we step away from the

Messiah, we will miss out on His blessings and experience the judgment of the living God.

To prove his point that the wilderness is normal and God delivers those with faith, the writer reminds his readers of the many heroes of faith who endured great difficulties but held on to God anyway (Hebrews 11). They are examples of those who inherit God's promises through faith and patience, without which entire generations can miss out on God's plan. So believers in Jesus should run with endurance, fixing their eyes only on Him, viewing God's discipline as proof that they are His children, and hanging on even when the entire world is shaking. Following Him will cost us practically everything, but it's worth everything and more. There is no way to please God without faith, the kind of faith that endures intense opposition and very long delays. Falling away is a return to Israel's tragic history. Enduring by faith is the key to blessings now and forever.

Nowhere in Scripture is faith more powerfully emphasized than in Hebrews. It's the assurance of what we hope for and the evidence of what we don't see. We're often surprised when our faith is tested, when circumstances contradict what God has said and the fulfillment of His promises lingers. The message of Hebrews and the rest of Scripture is that this is normal. This is the only way to align ourselves with God's purposes and enter into His rest. And this is the faith He rewards. When we stay the course and hang on to the way He is going, we experience His fulfillment. He has promised.

## QUESTIONS FOR REFLECTION

Why is endurance a necessary part of faith? Why do you think it's impossible to please God without faith?

DAY 82

# JAMES

A good seed planted in fertile ground under normal conditions won't simply remain a seed in the ground. It will grow into whatever it was destined to be. So when James speaks of the word that was planted in our hearts (James 1:21), it's no surprise that the following verses emphasize the fruit that it will produce. We receive the word by faith, but then it does something. It grows us into whatever we were destined to be.

Paul's message always emphasizes faith. James—not the disciple, but the half brother of Jesus and the leader of the Jerusalem church—puts a high premium on works. Because of that, many have seen a conflict between them, a between-the-lines argument in Scripture about the nature of salvation and the Christian life. James writes about how faith without works is dead—that even the demons believe God, which only makes them tremble. Head knowledge isn't enough. Real faith will always work its way outward and manifest in our lives.

Is this really a rebuttal of Paul? James and Paul already agreed on the nature of salvation and the Christian life at the council in Jerusalem (see Acts 15:1-29). They didn't leave that meeting on hostile terms. In fact, Paul himself knew there were distortions to his message—he addresses one of them in Romans 6—and James is probably responding to some of those same distortions. Yes, we are saved by grace through faith, but that isn't an opportunity for ungodly behavior. In fact, if it's true faith, Jesus really does live inside of us and His Spirit directs us from within. John will later say that those who belong to God can't continue to sin; the Spirit will point out sinful thoughts and behaviors, make sure we aren't content with them, and steadily change our nature. So faith that doesn't show itself in good works—not just avoiding sin but living for God's Kingdom and demonstrating His actions—isn't real faith at all. It's "dead and useless" (James 2:17).

James spends much of his letter discussing very practical aspects of the Christian life and what the Kingdom culture should look like. Christians should never show favoritism, as some in the church were doing. The rich had been seeing themselves as especially blessed, and the poor had seen themselves on the fringes, not only as the rabble of society but also as the rabble of the church. James corrects these misperceptions and does so with very severe words to the rich and proud. Christians must also learn how to tame their tongues because words are like a wildfire that can cause great destruction. The practice of faith affects our actions, our mouths, and our relationships. It's a deadly delusion to think that hearing and agreeing with God's Word is the same as doing it. A thousand messages from gifted teachers do no good if the truths learned from them don't produce change in our lives. We must be people who practice the wisdom that comes from God's Spirit and the humility that comes from knowing Him. God rejects the proud but shows favor to the humble. And when we pray as an earnest, righteous people, we have the same kind of powerful effect on God as Elijah had. These attitudes and actions are some of the fruits of real faith.

Like other New Testament writers, James contrasts our life in Jesus with the ways of the world. The letter begins with an encouraging statement about how trials and the testing of our faith produce endurance and character. Because of this we can even rejoice in the midst of our worst troubles, for they will produce eternal benefits in our lives. We can ask God for wisdom whenever we have these difficulties—or really anytime—and He will give it to us. But when the world puts pressure on us, many people tend to compromise in order to ease their suffering. That, says James, is a tragic response; friendship with the world is hostility toward God. With statements like these about suffering, endurance, faith, and compromise, we can assume that James, like Peter and the writer of Hebrews, feels the need to address a current persecution and urge Christians to withstand it. The fact that he is writing to Jewish believers who are already scattered among the nations fits this context. He is writing to Christians under stress.

But our faith always takes us deeper than the circumstances around us. No matter what obstacles we face, no matter what oppression we endure, no matter what crises rise up against us, God's wisdom and our faith are stronger and more lasting. Volatile surroundings are no match for God's peace and security. Our trust in Him produces maturity. We have no reason to be tossed in the waves and the wind. When we know that, we can face anything, not only with faith but also with pure joy.

## QUESTIONS FOR REFLECTION

Why do you think many people misunderstand the relationship between faith and works? How does James explain this relationship?

 DAY 83

# 1 PETER

Contrary to popular belief, there was never an empire-wide persecution against the early church. There were momentary, regional outbreaks—first in Jerusalem, later in Rome and other cities under emperors like Nero and Domitian—but no systematic attack on believers. The outbursts that did occur, however, were brutal at times. And more subtle forms of oppression, such as verbal attacks and discrimination, could be much more lasting and pervasive. Any time Christianity was seen as a threat to the public order—or to the divine order, as when Christians refused to worship the emperor or the pagan gods—local authorities could become oppressive. In volatile times, intense opposition can spring up at any moment.

Peter writes to Christians across the empire who are experiencing various degrees of suffering—some physically and violently, others more subtly—at the hands of specific opponents or the culture at large. He emphasizes the inheritance we have been given, an imperishable inheritance not rooted in this age, but eternal and certain. God has chosen us—Jewish and Gentile believers—as His royal nation of priests, His own possession that He is refining and preserving forever. When we suffer, we should not be surprised. Jesus Himself faced intense opposition, and God exalted Him. God allows our faith to be tested, knowing that it will prove to be pure gold. And when we endure unjust suffering, it's a testimony to those around us that we have a hope rooted in something deeper than our circumstances. Our trials may be painful, but they are temporary. Our salvation is forever.

As everlasting beings focused on the long view, we have a different outlook than the world on our relationships and how we conduct ourselves. Peter advises his readers about how to function in society, about having the right attitudes in marriage, being self-controlled, being holy as God is holy, forsaking pride and embracing humility, casting our anxieties on God, and resisting our adversary the devil. In every area, our lives are shaped by whether we have a here-and-now focus or a now-and-forever focus. It's vitally important to know who we are, who has called us, and where we're headed.

That's why we need to learn how to invest our thinking and our deepest hopes in the inheritance that can't pass away. We get glimpses of fulfilled hearts in this age, and God really does want us to experience His goodness in the land of the living (Psalm 27:13). But He has also subjected this world to futility so that we will seek something more (Romans 8:20-21). Though our salvation takes away much of that futility—it's not just a spiritual salvation, but includes degrees of emotional and physical healing—we still know what it means to be frustrated—always looking for that next level of fulfillment, but instead experiencing plans that don't work out, people who don't cooperate, and dreams that don't always become reality. When we fix our hope on the imperishable, our disappointments aren't quite so disappointing.

If salvation is our true focus, we really need to know what that salvation is. It isn't just floating around in heaven or being in a boring worship service forever. (Worship services in heaven are hardly boring—fire, lightning and thunder, unimaginably brilliant colors—but Scripture implies that heaven will be full of other activities and adventures too.) We will reign with Jesus in His Kingdom, which, from what we know of His creativity, will be bursting with life and excitement. Eternity will not be a letdown, as many seem to believe. It will be immensely worthwhile.

How do we respond to this eternal hope? By asking ourselves whether every passion, every activity, every investment of our time and resources really is valuable in the long run. Does it enhance the eternal future we want to have? When we look back on our earthly lives with regrets—"I wish I had relaxed and just enjoyed high school," "I wish I hadn't wasted so much money," "I wish I'd spent more time with my family rather than at the office"—these are really glimpses of a much greater dynamic on an eternal scale. In the fullness of God's Kingdom, we'll be glad for every investment we made in eternal matters. They will work out to our benefit as well as the benefit of others. One day, looking back, we will not regret whatever we had to endure today.

## QUESTIONS FOR REFLECTION

Why should we not be surprised when we encounter trials and testing? How does knowing our true identity and our future inheritance help us in difficult situations now?

DAY 84

# 2 PETER

Peter is in prison in Rome and expects to be executed soon. This isn't the first time his execution has been imminent—he was miraculously released from prison years before in Jerusalem—but this time his death seems certain. That is reason enough for his second letter to have a sense of urgency, though he may also be concerned for the critical problems facing the early church. Many false teachers have been influencing true believers with destructive heresies, teachings that are motivated by greed and filled with sensuality. These deceivers promise freedom but are themselves slaves of corruption, and all who embrace their words become corrupt too. Their teachings are seductive ideologies that will end with severe judgment for those who promote them.

Some Christians yearn for that judgment to come, while others are afraid of it because they don't want to be swept away with the wicked. Peter encourages both groups. To those who think that Jesus' return has been delayed way too long he says that God isn't slow at all. He's patient, and there's a world of difference between the two. He is giving more time for people to turn to Him. His Kingdom isn't yet as full as He wants it to be. It's good news that He hasn't come yet; we are waiting for new heavens and a new earth that is full of rightness and goodness and truth, a Kingdom that will have none of the brokenness we experience today. Things will work out there. Dreams will be fulfilled. People will get along and work seamlessly together. God is working toward this end, and being outside of time, He is in no hurry to resolve the issue. We may have to endure the scoffing of those who say He will never come, but His coming is nonetheless a certainty. In the end, God will prove Himself dramatically.

To those who fear God's judgment—not because they are outside of Christ but because they know how powerful His judgment can be—Peter says that God knows how to rescue the righteous in the midst of judgment. He rescued Noah and his family from the Flood, and He rescued Lot and his family from Sodom and Gomorrah. Those who are in a genuine relationship with Him have no need to worry.

In the meantime, God has given us the divine power needed for everything related to life and godliness. Not only that, He has given us the opportunity to share in His divine nature. We actually take on His life within us and grow to be like Him. He puts His own substance, His own self, inside of us. We can hardly imagine the full implications of this, but at the very least we can know that the power to be who we need to be and do what we need to do is already there. His great and precious promises have given us everything we need for every area of life.

This is why "I'm only human" is never an appropriate excuse for a Christian. If we mean "human" in the sense of being all that God intended His image-bearers to be, then it's true, though there's no "only" about it. But if we mean it as a rationale for why we fail so often, then what we really mean is, "I'm neglecting the divine nature God has given me because I don't fully believe it." That's not the sort of humanness we want. We are birthed into an eternal Kingdom by the perfect nature of an unimaginable power. We should never settle for any kind of existence that reflects less than that. If we embrace the divine qualities that Peter lists, even though we pursue them imperfectly, we can never be overcome by evil and will live in full confidence of our place in the eternal Kingdom.

## QUESTIONS FOR REFLECTION

What do you think it means to share in God's divine nature? Do you think Christians tend to make too much of this promise or too little of it? Why?

DAY 85

# 1 JOHN

The Gospel of John tells us about the light that came into the world and shone in the midst of darkness. John's first letter returns to that theme and urges followers of Jesus to come into the light and not remain in the dark. What does it mean to walk in the light? To practice the truth, to confess sin and be forgiven, to step out of sync with the world and its ways, to love others as God has loved us. These themes, which John explores and then comes back to again and again, are not only our goals; they are evidence of the nature put within us. This is how we know we are God's: We think, walk, and love like Jesus.

John begins his letter with an emphatic statement that he and others were eyewitnesses of the ministry of Jesus. It's uncertain why this is such an important point for John, but it's possible that some early form of Gnostic belief was infiltrating the church and convincing people that Jesus was only a spirit, that His works were mythically symbolic but not literal, that He didn't really die on the cross, or that He was only spiritually but not physically resurrected. Any of these claims would have provoked an intense reaction from a disciple who had seen Jesus firsthand and lived with Him for three years. And in the latter decades of the first century, there probably weren't many other eyewitnesses to refute such claims. So John writes from experience about the light that has come into the world, the nature of Jesus' love, and the kinds of works He did. Jesus, and God who sent Him, can be known. Literally.

We can also know whether we're in fellowship with God. If we say we love Him but hate others, we're lying. If our hearts don't condemn us, we have confidence before God. If we overcome the world through faith, we are born of Him. If we don't keep His commandments, we don't really love Him. These are strong words, but John has a gentle way of conveying them. And apparently this is a time for strong words. People have left the church (1 John 2:19). The spirit of the antichrist is already at work in the world, opposing God and seducing His people. The world is intoxicated with the evil one, and those who love the world and its ways are out of sync with God Himself. It's vitally important for followers of Jesus to test the spirits and know which beliefs are from God and which aren't. Those who confess that Jesus has come in the flesh—again, not as an illusion or only as a spirit, but in actual human form—have not been seduced by this false doctrine making its way through the culture. These are the ones who are of God and who overcome false testimonies.

John puts a lot of emphasis on living as Jesus lived and on loving in action rather than in words alone. John's words make the love of God seem warm and satisfying, but that isn't enough; real love must be expressed in deeds. God's love has miraculously transformed us into His children and, as God's children, we grow up to be a lot like Him. We're cut from the same cloth as our Father. The apples don't fall far from the tree in spiritual realms, just as in the natural world. If we are truly His, we can't persist in sin without being convinced that we are grieving Him and harming ourselves. We can't claim to be without sin, as some do, but neither can we continue in sin. We confess it and accept God's cleansing, which is thorough and complete. Then we are free to walk in the light He has given.

John has written to believers so that they may know they have eternal life (1 John 5:13), but this letter is more than just a reassurance about salvation. It's a description of the kind of eternal life we have. This life is relational, full of love and peace, transcending the world and its ways, practically relevant, and anchored in the truth of the incarnation of Jesus. And it's truer than any alternative we can ever be offered.

## QUESTIONS FOR REFLECTION

What does it mean to walk in the light as God is in the light? What are some of the ways we can do this?

 DAY 86

# 2 JOHN

John's second and third letters are very brief, and some say that both are written to individuals. But are "the chosen lady and . . . her children" (2 John 1:1) really an individual and her offspring? If so, the request in verse 5 to love one another comes across as rather odd, and the plural pronouns John uses throughout the letter seem unusual, as does his reference at the end to "the children of your sister" (2 John 1:13). It seems more likely that this letter is written to the bride of Christ and simply uses a Greek word for lady that was also commonly applied to social units in Greek cities. But regardless of the recipient, John's purposes are clear. He wants to stress many of the same themes he expressed in his longer letter.

These themes include the necessity of walking in truth, or "liv[ing] their lives as Jesus did," as John expressed it in his earlier letter (1 John 2:6). John often points out the connection between loving God and doing what He says. In his Gospel, he emphasizes this in the words of Jesus (John 14:15-24; 21:15-17), and his letters expand on the subject. John has noted that there are many in the world who "talk the talk" without "walking the walk." This is a strange phenomenon in every generation. We claim to be followers of Jesus and then don't imitate His lifestyle, attitudes, or actions very closely. What we generally mean is that we believe He will save us if we ask Him to, that we have chosen to side with

Him in the array of world religions, that we have chosen Him as the object of our spiritual desire. But actually following Him is another matter, and we often find ourselves neglecting huge portions of His words—the Sermon on the Mount, for example, or the radical expectations He has for how His disciples minister to others. When someone like Gandhi says he likes our Christ but not our Christianity, it's because there's a noticeable difference between Jesus' life and ours. And that's a problem that John repeatedly addresses in his letters.

The other extreme is to equate obedience with love and turn discipleship into a matter of doing the right things. While it's true that those who love Jesus will do what He says, it clearly isn't true that everyone who does what He says loves Him. Many people obey from a sense of guilt, some in an attempt to earn salvation, some from a sense of self-righteousness, some to fit into a religious culture, and some from a false sense of duty. None of these exemplify love, and God has made it clear that His greatest desire for us is that we love Him. So obedience is never enough, but love without doing what Jesus says isn't really love.

Doctrine isn't an expression of love either, even when it's right. But as is obvious from John's words in all of his letters, many teachers spread false beliefs in a spirit of self-promotion. Again, John urges his readers to watch out for those who deny that Jesus has come in the flesh. These are deceivers and antichrists, people who have departed from the teaching of Jesus. Not only should we reject their teachings, we shouldn't even show them hospitality, John says. We can assume that doesn't mean never having a conversation with cult members; it's clear in the New Testament that the early Christians were a part of an ongoing debate about matters of truth and error. But opening our minds to doctrines that deny Jesus or that distort who He is . . . well, that's pointless and even dangerous. John uses strong language in his plea for us to stay away from the seductions of false spirituality. Such teachings are wicked.

It is important to John that the "lady" who reads this letter, whether an individual or a church, be pure for her Bridegroom and share in His nature. This is God's desire for His people—not for them to be slavish "obeyers," but to be in sync with His heartbeat. The world and its deceptions are out of step with Him, but His people have a much higher calling. He wants nothing more than our full experience of His love and joy.

## Questions for Reflection

Do you think it's possible to love God without obeying Him? Is it possible to obey God without loving Him? Which is God's highest priority—our love or our obedience? Why?

 DAY 87

# 3 JOHN

Unlike the recipient of 2 John, the addressee of 3 John is specifically named. It's a dear friend of John's named Gaius, an example of what it means to walk in the light, the theme John continues to emphasize. Gaius has supported "brothers"—some people who have devoted themselves to the spread of the gospel—even though he hasn't known them personally. All he knows is that they are devoting themselves to "the Name" (3 John 1:7). And because he is a lover of that same Name, he is willing to support their work. Gaius's love is becoming known, and his reputation as a faithful man is being established.

Having commended Gaius, John rebukes an opponent by name and pledges to refute him in person when he comes to visit. This teacher, Diotrephes, loves to put himself first. He doesn't accept John's authority and slanders the apostle, as well as others. He apparently has some authority or role as a leader, as he refuses to welcome John's friends and tries to put them out of the church. He is an example of prideful, self-serving leadership—which unfortunately is not unique to the first century. John believes such pride should be pointed out and publicly addressed.

Then John calls out a good example, a man named Demetrius, who does what is good and has earned a good reputation. This is what John has been talking about—that those who do good and those who do evil reveal their relationship with God by their works.

Unlike Paul's letters to individuals, 3 John contains very little instruction. His primary purpose in writing is to send his greetings and express his desire to visit. This correspondence is a glimpse into the kinds of relationships that developed among first-century Christians—personal, affectionate, and forged in the fire of a hostile environment. Not all churches faced persecution, but all faced false teachings and misunderstandings. Christians were a small minority in most places. Such conditions create strong bonds.

These conditions also have a way of refining what we believe. Sometimes the narrow place of faith in a difficult environment causes people to walk away; with others, it causes them to draw much closer to God and to each other. These are the dynamics we see not only in John's letters, but in Paul's and Peter's as well. The culture is a strange stew of beliefs and attitudes, and maintaining Christian beliefs and Christlike attitudes and actions isn't easy. That's why John spends so much time describing the lifestyle of a Jesus-follower and urging his readers to know the nature of what they believe and the One they serve. It's also why he gives instructions about whom to support and whom to avoid. Those who work for truth are worthy of support. Those who don't—or who use truth for their own self-promotion—are not. It's that simple. In an age of widely conflicting ideas and worldviews, it's important to be vigilant about truth in one's own life and in the culture at large.

But the truth John defends is never simply a doctrinal issue. It's a relational issue. Jesus *is* the truth, and we can only live in the light by knowing Him. Furthermore, we can only experience Jesus by knowing His love, not by getting our doctrine right. This is a gospel of relationship, not of arguments. We discern the Spirit of Jesus and the spirit of the antichrist by our spiritual senses and simply by being led. Only those who cling to Jesus and who are bathed in His love can live in truth.

## QUESTIONS FOR REFLECTION

How would you describe someone who walks in the light and follows Jesus closely? What attitudes does he or she have? What kinds of works does he or she do? How well does this description line up with your life right now?

 DAY 88

# JUDE

Like James, Jude is a half brother of Jesus who apparently accepted Him only after His death and resurrection. His short letter to the church is a scathing judgment against false teachers. He says he is contending for the faith, and it's true, for this is a very contentious letter. It refers to deceivers who have crept into the fellowship of believers, who pervert God's grace and use it as an excuse for sensuality and deny Jesus as Master and Lord. They are hidden dangers at Christian feasts and fellowships, people whom Jude compares to shepherds feeding themselves, clouds without water, trees without fruit at harvest time, breaking waves of the sea, and stars wandering in utter darkness. And as Jude makes clear, they are destined for a very harsh judgment.

Jude is one of the least-read New Testament letters for several reasons: its brevity—only twenty-five verses; its harsh tone; the fact that portions of the letter are a near duplication of 2 Peter (either Jude quotes Peter at length or Peter quotes Jude at length); and the fact that Jude quotes non-scriptural Jewish books such as 1 Enoch and the Assumption (or Testament) of Moses. On this last issue, no one seems to know what to do with a Spirit-inspired writer who uses somewhat spurious literature to make a point. It's true that Paul quotes pagan poets at times, but not on details regarding God's history with His people. And it's true that the Spirit could have preserved accurate ancient traditions for several centuries and inspired the writers of myth-based apocryphal literature to incorporate them in their works. Regardless, it's easy enough to say that the quotes from 1 Enoch and the Assumption of Moses are reliable while the sources as a whole are not, and this is where most Christians leave it. Jude is drawing from his culture to express eternal truth.

The letter is entirely focused on the false teaching, which apparently promotes licentiousness in the name of grace. Our culture can relate quite easily to this problem; many claim to follow Jesus while engaging in actions that physically contradict His purposes. This happens in a sex-saturated culture—Jude's references to the days of Noah and to Sodom and Gomorrah are intentionally loaded with meaning—with the result that people try to separate their spiritual lives from their morality so they can have both the eternal salvation of the gospel and the pleasures of their immediate passions. Of course, the true gospel covers every area of life, so no such dichotomy is legitimate. Either we express the faithfulness and character and purity of God spiritually, emotionally, physically, and relationally or we don't. He forgives us when we fail, but

He doesn't give us permission to willfully divide up our lives and only follow Him in parts of them. Jude and other New Testament writers condemn such distortions of the truth.

Jude's primary rationale is that the compassionate, loving, gracious Jesus has also judged people harshly throughout history. We may be surprised that Jude says Jesus delivered God's people out of Egypt, but it was normal for the early church to see Him working throughout world history and Israel's story. It's possible to see Jesus as the priest who visited Abraham, the angel who wrestled with Jacob, the angel who visited Joshua, the fourth man in the fiery furnace in Babylon, and so on. He has always been active in creation, world history, and Jewish history—at times as a judge of those who rebel and refuse to believe the truth. So we are to see in Him both the kindness and the severity of God, as Paul puts it in Romans 11:22.

But for those who believe, we are to build ourselves up in faith and have mercy on those who doubt. God is able to keep us from stumbling and to preserve us as blameless until Jesus returns. His work in us is certain, even amidst the turmoil of a truth-impaired world. When we seek God's truth alone—to know it and to live it out—He leads us into it and keeps us completely safe in Jesus.

## Questions for Reflection

Do you think Jude's harsh words about those who pervert the gospel of grace—using it as an excuse for sensuality—are relevant today? Why or why not? How is Jesus an expression of both the kindness and the severity of God?

DAY 89

# REVELATION 1–3

John, who wrote the Gospel and the three letters, is exiled on the island of Patmos, not far from the coast of Asia Minor and the city of Ephesus. He lived in Ephesus at times and ministered to the churches there and in nearby cities. He gives no reason for his exile, other than being sent there for his testimony during a time of suffering, and we don't know whether it's during the reign of Nero in the 60s or Domitian in the 90s. All we know is that while the church is under duress, Jesus gives John a vision of things that "must soon take place" (Revelation 1:1), launching into a sweeping picture behind the scenes of the natural world. The veil is lifted to reveal the throne room of God, the activities of multitudes of angels and demons, the workings of the archenemy, Satan, the trials and tribulations that will come on the world, and the ultimate victory that Jesus has won and that His people will enjoy forever. This picture is meant to comfort Christians who are being persecuted and who may believe, because of outward appearances, that evil is winning. Clearly, when the big picture is revealed, evil is not even remotely close to winning. In fact, it is in the process of being utterly destroyed.

But the book doesn't begin with this full cosmic display. John introduces his vision, which begins with a dramatic encounter with Jesus, who tells him to write what he sees and send it to seven churches in the cities on the nearby mainland. The next two chapters encapsulate the messages to these seven churches. In most, Jesus begins with a commendation, offers some words of correction, and ends with more encouraging words, including some that promise a reward for those who will hear and obey. (His messages to Smyrna and Philadelphia contain no rebukes, and His message to Laodicea contains no commendation.) These messages are filled with implicit references to the cultural and geographical context of the cities. It is clear that the churches are under some form of persecution or are contending with some form of false teaching or temptation to compromise. Some are strong and zealous; others are weak and apathetic. But all are under the watchful eye of Jesus Himself.

Even though these messages were intended for specific churches that ceased to exist long ago, they contain powerful messages for us today. They tell us that God is sovereign over our circumstances; that He lets Satan inflict pain on His people, but limits it when He chooses to; that He lets Satan try to seduce His people, but gives them the power to remain pure and faithful; that He puts a high premium on faith and endurance; and that suffering is short-term, while the Kingdom and its rewards are forever. This section concludes with a highly relevant appeal to any and every church: Those who hear Jesus knocking and open the door to Him will enjoy fellowship with Him. This plea seems to be framed in the context of churches inviting Him into their communion meals, but it's applied much more broadly than that. This is a clear statement of God's desire to have intimate fellowship with His people. He wants closeness, and those who respond to His desire will enjoy His fullness.

That and other rewards offered to these churches are given to those who overcome. These rewards include surviving the last death; eating from the tree of life in God's paradise; being sustained by hidden manna; receiving the blessing of a new name, white garments, and an indelible name in the Book of Life; becoming a pillar in the new Jerusalem; having authority over the nations; and sitting with Jesus on His throne. These are extravagant promises, but they are conditional on our faithfulness in the midst of all kinds of testings and temptations. They are promised not to the perfect but to overcomers—those who endure, who come out of the melee of this world with their faith intact, who face vicious spiritual adversaries and cling to Jesus anyway. Yes, we stumble and fall at times, but God declares victory if we get back up and simply remain in Him. Perseverance is a profound spiritual virtue, and God rewards it highly. His desire for fellowship with us is fulfilled when we overcome every obstacle that stands in the way of it.

## QUESTIONS FOR REFLECTION

What do you think it means to overcome? What promises does Jesus give to those who do?

 DAY 90

# REVELATION 4–22

It's hard to imagine any book of Scripture being interpreted in more diverse ways than the book of Revelation. John's vision seems at times a perfect symbolic description of the reign of Nero and those who succeed him up through the fall of Jerusalem. At other times, the vision seems clearly more cosmic and comprehensive than that. We know the beginning addresses several specific churches of John's era, and we know the end describes the final destination of God's people and His decisive victory over evil. We see the immediate and the ultimate in these verses, as well as lots of enigmatic pictures in between. These images raise as many questions as they answer.

We do learn quite a few things with certainty, however. For one, God's throne room is an exciting place to be. There are throngs of people, flashes of lightning and rumblings of thunder, colors and textures that John strains to describe, majesty that can hardly be conveyed, and ultimate honor given to Jesus, the Lamb of God and King of kings. We also see that the events of earth have always been shaped by a cosmic rebellion against God, and that God has defeated this rebellion through Jesus and will finally put an end to it in the most emphatic terms. The enemy hasn't given up his fight, but God hasn't yet unleashed His full judgment either. The world's corrupt systems—with all their greed, injustice, and unholy agendas—will be completely undone in a staggeringly short time, and Satan will be cast into a lake of fire. There will be battles and plagues along the way—some of them fierce and devastating—though there's no doubt about the outcome, for Jesus has sealed the victory. But until that victory fully appears, many nations will be deceived and many of God's people will have to suffer and hang on tightly to the truth.

As Jesus made clear to the seven churches in the first three chapters of the book, the rewards for hanging on are extravagant. The last chapters of Revelation describe a wedding between Jesus and His people; a new Jerusalem coming down from heaven and a temple filled with the presence of God; full access to the tree of life; every tear being wiped away, and unbridled jubilation throughout all of creation. God is making all things new, and everyone who is thirsty enough to come to Him can enjoy His living waters forever.

Quoting the prophet Isaiah, Paul once wrote that no eye has seen what God has prepared for those who love Him. In fact, no mind has even conceived of it. That tells us that we will all be surprised in heaven because it's more than we could ever imagine. Whatever we've envisioned falls short of reality. That's almost always the case with God's plans, even the ones that will be fulfilled in our lives on earth, but especially with the final fulfillment. God won't simply return us to our condition in Eden before the Fall. He will make things even better. We will not be disappointed.

That's why the book of Revelation ends with a plea for Jesus to come. We long for a Savior who will make everything right, mainly because we're fully aware of how much can go wrong in this world. We're grateful for the salvation He accomplished, the Spirit He filled us with, and the purpose and meaning He has given our lives. But sometimes life hurts, and we yearn for a day when it won't. According to the promise of Revelation, that day is coming as stealthily as a thief in the night. The Spirit and the bride invite us to come, and we invite Jesus to come. This is truly a match made in heaven, and it will be everything our hearts desire.

## QUESTIONS FOR REFLECTION

Why is it important for us to know the end of the story while we're living in the middle of it? How does the picture of fulfillment in Revelation 21–22 shape our lives today?

# 🍂 CONCLUSION

This epic story that began with a beautiful creation getting ugly has ended with restoration and fulfillment beyond our dreams. The broken has been repaired, and the corruption has been cleansed. Justice has been served, and mercy has triumphed. Along the way, we have seen God's relentless search for closeness with His people, and His people falteringly, imperfectly, but eventually, responding. He has taken us from being wanderers to being tentative followers to being servants to being children and a bride. The depths we sank to and the heights to which we have been lifted are, at both extremes, astonishing. From God's perspective, this story is the greatest love story ever conceived—that of a King who comes to rescue His bride and woo her into His arms. From a human perspective, it's the ultimate rags-to-riches story—about orphans and rebels who have nevertheless been chosen as children and intimate partners of the King Himself. The key variable in all of Scripture is who responds and who doesn't. Those who respond have looked past all the lies and obstacles, recognized the King's heart and His intentions, embraced His goodness, and said yes to Him by faith.

The centerpiece of this story is the incarnation of the King and, even more specifically, His sacrificial death and resurrection. Without this, there is no restoration. No penalty has been paid, justice falls unyieldingly on the guilty, and we are left with nothing but an impossibly high standard we can never live up to, an infinite debt we can never pay. This rescue is enormously costly to the King, but He gladly pays the cost for the joy it will bring Him. It's costly for us, too—we give up everything to follow Him—but there's a joy set before us as well. Jesus gives us His life in exchange for ours, a better deal than we've ever been offered. The end result is an intimate union that goes even deeper than God's fellowship with His first image-bearers in Eden.

This is the motive behind Creation, the guiding purpose behind the human story, and the destiny that will continue to shape us throughout eternity. In other words, this is what we were made for. God Himself ensures that this purpose and destiny will be fulfilled if we accept His pursuit of our hearts. The persistent invitation of Scripture is for us to do exactly that. Our part in the story depends on what we do with that invitation.

# Appendix

*Discussion Questions for Small Groups*

Though this book is designed primarily as a personal devotional, it can also be used in small groups as a thirteen-week overview of Scripture. For your convenience, we have gathered the Questions for Reflection from each of the ninety days into thirteen sessions here. In order to make each session a cohesive unit—not splitting any books of the Bible between two sessions, for example—not every week will focus on exactly seven readings. Some will cover six or eight readings, and group participants will need to adjust accordingly if they have been using the readings as daily devotionals. After thirteen weeks of discussion, participants will have a better grasp of the unity and completeness of God's Word.

## Session 1

*The Old Testament:* What first comes to mind when you think of the Old Testament? How important do you think it is to our understanding of the New Testament? Why?

*Genesis 1–3:* How did God demonstrate in Genesis that He had already planned a solution for humanity's fall? Do you think God already has solutions for the crises we face today? Why or why not?

*Genesis 4–11:* In what ways does Genesis 4–11 reflect the truth of Romans 8:20-21?

*Genesis 12–24:* In what ways do you relate to Abraham and Sarah's long wait for a fulfilled promise? What temptations did they face in the process? What similar temptations have you faced, and how have you overcome them?

*Genesis 25–36:* In what ways do you relate to Jacob's wrestling match with God? Why do you think God invites us to interact with Him like that? In what ways does it encourage you that God's chosen people in Genesis were at times examples of extreme dysfunction? How does this challenge modern perceptions of the kinds of people God chooses to work through?

*Genesis 37–50:* In what ways do you relate to Joseph's trials? How do you respond to being treated unfairly? How easily do you express forgiveness? How does knowing that God is ultimately in charge of your life make it easier to forgive others and trust Him in the midst of difficult circumstances?

## Session 2

*Exodus 1–15:* What does the Exodus show us about God's nature? What aspects of His nature did Israel experience? What aspects of God's nature do you experience when you're in need?

*Exodus 16–34:* Why do you think the Israelites struggled with faith even after seeing dramatic miracles such as the ten plagues and the parting of the Red Sea? How did God feel about their complaints in the wilderness? In what ways are you tempted to complain about the ways God deals with you?

*Exodus 35–40:* How did the Israelites respond to God's presence? In what ways do you think God wants to make His presence known in your life? Why do you think God's guidance of Israel (a cloud by day and a pillar of fire by night that could move at any time) was unpredictable? What does that tell us about how He leads us?

*Leviticus:* What relevance does Leviticus have for us today? What do the details about worship and purity tell us about what God desires for His people?

*Numbers 1–10:* In what ways are we living between our deliverance and our Promised Land? What aspects of the wilderness experience can you relate to?

*Numbers 11–36:* Why do you think God reacted so harshly to the Israelites' complaints? Why did their lack of faith cause a generation to miss out on something God had promised?

*Deuteronomy:* What is God's primary purpose for us? What are the obligations of being in this kind of relationship? What are the benefits?

## Session 3

*Joshua:* What "territory" do you think God wants you to take for His Kingdom? for your family? in your work? What truths from Joshua will be most helpful as you do that?

*Judges:* Have you seen the "Judges cycle" at work in your life? If so, how has God delivered you when you've cried out to Him? What does the book of Judges tell us about the kinds of people God works through?

*Ruth:* In what ways is the story of Ruth and Boaz a picture of our relationship with Jesus?

*1 Samuel:* Why do you think there's such a long gap between David's anointing as king and the time when Saul dies and David actually becomes king? What do you think God accomplished during these years?

*2 Samuel:* What does it mean to be someone after God's own heart? What did that look like in David's life? What does it look like in yours?

*1 Kings:* How do you think someone as wise as Solomon ended up disillusioned and depressed? Why did his wisdom not lead to fulfillment and satisfaction?

*2 Kings:* How do you think you would have responded to prophets such as Elijah and Elisha? What do they tell us about the way God speaks? What do their interactions with Israel tell us about the way people respond?

# SESSION 4

*1 Chronicles:* Why do you think David was so passionate about his desire to build a temple? What did he want for it to accomplish?

*2 Chronicles:* Why is worship such a critical issue in Scripture? Why did Israel keep turning to idols? How did God keep prompting them to turn back to Him? What does worship of God accomplish in our lives?

*Ezra:* Have you experienced God as a restorer? If so, how? What have you learned about Him in the restoration process? How has it changed you and deepened your relationship with Him?

*Nehemiah:* What does Nehemiah teach us about persistence in accomplishing God's will? What does he teach us about handling conflict and eliminating distractions? Why are these things necessary in our walk with God?

*Esther:* In what ways do we have to "read between the lines" of our lives to see God? Do you tend to see circumstances as arranged by God or as the results of human decisions—or both? Why?

*Job:* Under what circumstances are you most likely to question God's goodness? Why must our worship of Him never be contingent on circumstances? Why is it wrong to apply uniform scriptural explanations to the trials we or others face?

# SESSION 5

*Psalms 1–41:* What do the Psalms tell us about the ways we approach God and the attitudes we're allowed to bring with us? Why do you think God inspired psalms that express such a wide range of human emotion?

*Psalms 42–72:* How honest are you with God in your prayers? In what ways can the Psalms help us pray when we don't know what to say to God?

*Psalms 73–89:* When is a lament spiritually helpful, and when is it a distortion of God's hope? How can we lament appropriately without slipping into harmful negativity?

*Psalms 90–106:* What happens inside of us when we worship in spite of apparent contradictions in our lives or in the midst of deep pain? Why are joy, gratitude, and praise appropriate in any situation?

*Psalms 107–150:* In what sense are the messianic prophecies in the Psalms an answer to the needs and desires expressed in each psalm?

*Proverbs:* Why is it dangerous to view the Proverbs as rigid, unbending principles that are always proven true? In what ways can they (and any other section of Scripture) become a substitute for our relationship with God? How should we apply them to our lives?

*Ecclesiastes:* In what ways does Ecclesiastes point us to Jesus? How is it a reflection of some of the philosophies and lifestyles of our own era?

*Song of Songs:* As an expression of marital sex and pleasure, what does the Song reveal about God and His personality? As an allegory of our relationship with God, what does the Song say about Him?

## SESSION 6

*Isaiah 1–39:* In what ways does the book of Isaiah reflect the Bible as a whole? Why is it quoted so often in the New Testament?

*Isaiah 40–59:* What do Isaiah's predictions of restoration and of the Messiah tell us about God's sovereignty over history? How do they serve as evidence of who Jesus is? In what ways is the hope of these chapters relevant to your current needs and circumstances?

*Isaiah 60–66:* What role do we play in God's coming Kingdom? In what ways can we "arise" and "shine" with God's glory on us? What do you think God means by "new heavens and a new earth" in Isaiah 65:17?

*Jeremiah 1–29:* Why is the mission to represent God's heart not always a pleasant one? Why didn't God give Jeremiah a more fulfilling task? Does the picture of God grieving and feeling pain change your perception of Him? Why or why not?

*Jeremiah 30–52:* Why is a new heart necessary for us to love and follow God?

*Lamentations:* Why do you think God had Jeremiah preach when He knew His people wouldn't listen? In the midst of our hardest times, worst failures, and deepest pain, why is it important to remember that God's mercies are new every morning? How can we experience His new mercies?

*Ezekiel 1–39:* How does the image of God breathing life into dry bones to re-create His people reveal His message more powerfully than simply telling us He is a restorer? Has God used visual illustrations of His truth in your life? If so, how have they affected you?

*Ezekiel 40–48:* What aspects of God's restoration process for His creation can only be accomplished by Him? What aspects can we participate in now?

## Session 7

*Daniel 1–6:* How can we know when it's okay to adapt to our culture and when we should remain uncompromising? What does Daniel's example teach us about standing firm for what we believe? Do you believe Daniel's ability to hear God and receive His wisdom is an example for us or an exception that we can't follow? Why?

*Daniel 7–12:* Why do you think Daniel prayed and fasted when he learned of Jeremiah's prophecy that the captivity would last for only seventy years? Do you tend to see God's promises as inevitable, or do you think we are supposed to pray for their fulfillment and receive them by faith? Why?

*Hosea:* Why is unfaithfulness to God considered adultery? Why do you think the people of Israel kept turning their hearts to lesser gods? In what ways do we do that today?

*Joel:* What conditions does God place on His people in order for them to have a meaningful, vibrant relationship with Him? What role does repentance play in preparing for or preserving that relationship?

*Amos:* How concerned do you think most Christians are about the issues in Amos—specifically oppression, injustice, exploitation of the poor, and similar social issues? Why? How does God want us to deal with such issues today?

*Obadiah:* How does the principle that we reap what we sow apply to us in light of our salvation? How can we use that principle to our benefit?

*Jonah:* Why did God want Jonah to share His heart for the Ninevites? Why was that difficult for Jonah? In what ways does God want us to share His heart today? In what ways is that difficult for you? Why?

## SESSION 8

*Micah:* What are the spiritual dangers of living in a complacent, prosperous society? Why do you think many Christians tend to see sexual immorality as more sinful than ethical immorality?

*Nahum:* How do you feel when you read headlines that show the world as unstable and threatening? How easy or difficult is it for you to rest in God's sovereignty over global events?

*Habakkuk:* How do you think Habakkuk was able to settle the question of God's goodness in his heart? What was the key to finding joy in spite of circumstances?

*Zephaniah:* To what degree do you think today's church is spiritually complacent? Why is complacency such a dangerous condition? How does it affect you to know that God holds His people in His arms and sings over them?

*Haggai:* What are some actions or attitudes in our lives that demonstrate our level of hunger for God's presence? What can we do to position ourselves to experience more of His presence? How do you think God responds when we clearly prioritize Him in every area of life?

*Zechariah:* How does it make you feel to know that God burns with jealousy over the inclination of your heart? What needs to happen in our hearts for God's desire for us to be satisfied?

*Malachi:* In what ways, if any, have you been disappointed with God's work in your life? What do you think God would say about your disappointments? In what ways, and to what degree, do our responses to God determine our experience of Him?

# SESSION 9

*The New Testament:* In what ways do you crave meaning and purpose in life? How have you longed for God to show Himself in your life and make things right? Why do you think God sometimes waits so long to fulfill His promises?

*Matthew 1–16:* What aspects of God's Kingdom do you long for most? How is Jesus working His Kingdom into your life? How is He working it into the world around you?

*Matthew 17–28:* In what ways are the values of Jesus' Kingdom radically different from the values of this world? How difficult is it to live by Kingdom values while we live in the world? How can we embody the Good News?

*Mark:* In what situations do you need to hear Jesus say, "Don't be afraid—just believe"? Why is this command appropriate in almost every area of our lives? Why do you think God made faith such a necessary aspect of relating to Him?

*Luke: The Ministry of Jesus:* How does following Jesus change the way we see people? How does it change the way we see the world?

*Luke: The Parables of Jesus:* How do Jesus' parables change the way we understand prayer? How do they change the way we see ourselves as God's children?

*John 1–12:* In what ways is John the most intensely relational Gospel? What does it show us about God's desire to be known?

*John 13–21:* What are the implications of "being one with Jesus" in our attitudes and emotions? in our actions? in our relationships? How can we draw our life from Him?

## SESSION 10

*Acts 1–12:* How can we balance the need to make plans in our lives with the need to respond to the Holy Spirit's leading? How do we know when to change directions to follow Him? Why is it important to be empowered by the Spirit?

*Acts 13–28:* How open are you to being surprised by the Holy Spirit's direction? In what ways has He reshaped your thinking in the past? How long does it normally take for you to adjust to Him?

*Romans 1–8, 12–16:* Why is it necessary to consider ourselves dead and resurrected with Jesus—that is, for the Holy Spirit to be the source of life within us? How can we distinguish outward obedience produced by our own efforts to obey God from inward obedience produced by the transforming power of the Holy Spirit in our lives?

*Romans 9–11:* What promises are you waiting for God to fulfill? What encouragement does the letter to the Romans offer when you experience delays or when it seems as if God is not coming through for you?

*1 Corinthians:* To what extent does love—the kind of love Paul describes in 1 Corinthians 13—resolve virtually all of the relational problems we have? Why is this kind of love so rare and so difficult to practice?

*2 Corinthians:* How do our current troubles produce an eternal glory in us? Why can we be confident that our weaknesses are not a hindrance to God's power working within us?

*Galatians:* What is the difference between living by the Spirit and living by the flesh? Why don't we need to worry that living by the Spirit instead of the law will lead to unrighteousness?

## SESSION 11

*Ephesians:* Why is it hard to believe extreme statements about our life in Christ—such as our being seated with Him in heavenly places or being filled with God's fullness? How can we experience these truths in practical ways?

*Philippians:* How can we have joy in all circumstances? How can we have peace in trying times? What will humility accomplish in our relationships with God and with others?

*Colossians:* How does setting our minds on things above and fixing our eyes on Jesus accomplish what we need spiritually? How does this approach to spiritual growth help satisfy God's desire for closeness with us?

*1 Thessalonians:* How does our hope for Jesus' return shape how we live now? What does it mean for our work? our purity? our long-term relationships?

*2 Thessalonians:* How can we balance being ready for Jesus' return with being responsible in planning for the future? Why is patience such an important attribute in God's Kingdom?

*1 Timothy:* Do you think some Christians and churches today divide over distracting details and get caught up in pointless arguments? Why or why not? What do you think are the essential beliefs Christians must agree on?

*2 Timothy:* How do the illustrations of a soldier, an athlete, and a farmer help us stay focused on what's most important? Why do we need to eliminate distractions in our spiritual lives?

## SESSION 12

*Titus:* Are there any ways in which you're tempted to compartmentalize your life and leave God out of certain aspects of it? If so, what can you do to embrace a fuller, more holistic salvation?

*Philemon:* In what ways is the story of Onesimus a picture of the gospel?

*Hebrews:* Why is endurance a necessary part of faith? Why do you think it's impossible to please God without faith?

*James:* Why do you think many people misunderstand the relationship between faith and works? How does James explain this relationship?

*1 Peter:* Why should we not be surprised when we encounter trials and testing? How does knowing our true identity and our future inheritance help us in difficult situations now?

*2 Peter:* What do you think it means to share in God's divine nature? Do you think Christians tend to make too much of this promise or too little of it? Why?

## SESSION 13

*1 John:* What does it mean to walk in the light as God is in the light? What are some of the ways we can do this?

*2 John:* Do you think it's possible to love God without obeying Him? Is it possible to obey God without loving Him? Which is God's highest priority—our love or our obedience? Why?

*3 John:* How would you describe someone who walks in the light and follows Jesus closely? What attitudes does he or she have? What kinds of works does he or she do? How well does this description line up with your life right now?

*Jude:* Do you think Jude's harsh words about those who pervert the gospel of grace by using it as an excuse for sensuality are relevant today? Why or why not? How is Jesus an expression of both the kindness and the severity of God?

*Revelation 1–3:* What do you think it means to overcome? What promises does Jesus give to those who do?

*Revelation 4–22:* Why is it important for us to know the end of the story while we're living in the middle of it? How does the picture of fulfillment in Revelation 21–22 shape our lives today?

# About Walk Thru the Bible

For more than three decades, Walk Thru the Bible has been dedicated to igniting a passion for God's Word worldwide through live events, devotional magazines, and resources designed for both small groups and individual use. Known for innovative methods and high-quality resources, we serve the whole body of Christ across denominational, cultural, and national lines.

Walk Thru the Bible communicates the truths of God's Word in a way that makes the Bible readily accessible to anyone. We are committed to developing user-friendly resources that are Bible centered, of excellent quality, life changing for individuals, and catalytic for churches, ministries, and movements; and we are committed to maintaining our global reach through strategic partnerships while adhering to the highest levels of integrity in all we do.

Walk Thru the Bible partners with the local church worldwide to fulfill its mission, helping people "walk thru" the Bible with greater clarity and understanding. Live events and small group curricula are taught in over 45 languages by more than 30,000 instructors in more than 104 countries, and more than 100 million devotionals have been packaged into daily magazines, books, and other publications that reach over 5 million people each year.

Walk Thru the Bible
www.walkthru.org
1-800-361-6131

# About the Author

**Chris Tiegreen** has inspired thousands of people through *The One Year At His Feet Devotional, The One Year Walk with God Devotional, The One Year Worship the King Devotional, The One Year Wonder of the Cross Devotional,* and *The One Year Experiencing God's Presence Devotional,* as well as through his books *Unburdened, Fixing Abraham, Feeling like God, Violent Prayer,* and *Creative Prayer.* His experiences as a missionary, pastor, journalist, and university instructor bring a unique perspective to his writing. He is currently an editor at Walk Thru the Bible.

# Online Discussion *guide*

## Take *your* TYNDALE READING EXPERIENCE *to the* NEXT LEVEL

---

A FREE discussion guide for this book is available at bookclubhub.net, perfect for sparking conversations in your book group or for digging deeper into the text on your own.

## www.bookclubhub.net

*You'll also find free discussion guides for other Tyndale books, e-newsletters, e-mail devotionals, virtual book tours, and more!*